*コミュニケーション活動や英作文で活用しましょう。
*カタカナを参考に発音して，どんどん使ってみましょう。
*使えるようになった語句・表現には，☐ に印をつけましょう。
*さらに知りたい語句・表現は，先生に質問したり辞書を使って調べたりしましょう。

Part 2　学校生活

Topic 9	学校で At School ································· 24
Topic 10	授業やテストについて話そう！ What Is Your Favorite Subject? ············· 26
Topic 11	部活動について話そう！ What Club Are You In? ······················ 28
Topic 12	友だちや先生について話そう！ Your Friends and Teachers ················ 30
Topic 13	修学旅行や林間学校について話そう！ Let's Talk about School Trips! ········ 32
Topic 14	体育祭や合唱祭について話そう！ Field Day and Chorus Contest ··········· 34

Part 3　場面

Topic 15	買い物に行こう！ Let's Go Shopping! ······························ 36
Topic 16	電話でデートに誘おう！ Talking on the Phone ······················· 38
Topic 17	道案内をしよう！ Asking the Way ································ 40
Topic 18	困難を切り抜けよう！ Let's Overcome Our Difficulties! ················ 42

付　録

1	人に関する表現 ·· 44
2	物を表す表現 ··· 45
3	生き物や食べ物 ·· 46
4	動作を表す言葉（動詞）·· 48

Let's Start 1 — Classroom English
授業で使える英語

●名前を呼ばれたとき，手を挙げるとき

- ☐ Here!（はい！）
- ☐ ～ is absent.（～はお休みです） エアブスント

●相手の言うことが聞き取れないとき

- ☐ Please speak more slowly. スロウリィ
  （もっとゆっくり話してください）
- ☐ Please speak a little louder. ラウダァ
  （もう少し大きな声で話してください）

●聞き返すとき

- ☐ Once more, please. ゥワンス
  （もう一度お願いします）
- ☐ Excuse me? イクスキューズ
- ☐ Pardon me? パードンヌ
  （すみませんが，何て言ったのですか）

●相手の英語が分からないとき

- ☐ What does ～ mean? ミーンズ
  （～はどういう意味ですか）
- ☐ What is ～ in Japanese?
  （～は日本語で何と言いますか）

★他にもこんな言い方があるよ！

- ☐ Will you say that again?（もう一度言ってください）
- ☐ What did you say?（何て言ったの？）
- ☐ Give me a hint, please.（ヒントをください）
- ☐ Give me an example, please. イグゼアムプウ（例を挙げてください）
- ☐ I know. Please ask me!（答えられるので当ててください）
- ☐ Please help me.（助けてください）
- ☐ I'm sorry. I forgot. フォガット（すみませんが，忘れてしまいました）

Let's Start

★授業でたくさん使ってみよう！
英語の授業では，いろいろな表現を英語で言えるようにしておくといいですよ。
困ったときも，英語で切り抜ける裏わざを身につけておけば大丈夫！

●質問するとき

☐ Excuse me. May I ask a question?
（すみませんが，質問してもいいですか）

●ちょっと待ってほしいとき

☐ Well ...（ええと）
☐ Let me see ...（ええと）
☐ Just a moment, please.
（モウマント）
（ちょっと待ってください）

●答えられないとき

☐ I'm sorry. I don't know.
☐ I'm sorry. I don't understand.
（アンダスタンド）
（すみませんが，分かりません）

●英語が思い浮かばないとき

☐ How do you say ～ in English?
☐ What is ～ in English?
（～は英語で何と言いますか）
☐ I'm sorry. I don't know how to say it in English.
（すみません。英語でどう言うのか分かりません）

●相手の考えに賛成したり反対したりするとき

☐ I think so, too. （私もそう思います）
☐ I don't think so. （私はそうは思いません）

☐ How do you read [pronounce] this word?（この単語はどう読む[発音する]んですか）
（プゥラナウンス）
☐ How do you spell ～?（～はどうつづるんですか）
☐ May I answer in Japanese?（日本語で答えてもいいですか）
☐ I'm not sure, but I think ...（自信はないけれど，…だと思います）
（シュア）
☐ Just a minute.（ちょっと待って）
（ミネイト）
☐ Please wait.（待ってください）
☐ I'm sorry. I have no idea.（すみませんが，さっぱり分かりません）
（アイディア）

Let's Start 2 — Classroom English
いろいろな場面で使える便利な表現 1

● あいづちを打つ

- ☐ Really?（本当に？）
- ☐ Are you serious?（マジで？）スィゥリァス
- ☐ Aha. / Uh-huh. / Um. / Hum.（ふーん）
- ☐ I see. / I got it.（分かったよ）
- ☐ Do you? / Are you? / Did you?（へえ，そうなんだぁ）
- ☐ Sure. Of course.（もちろん）アブ コース
- ☐ No wonder.（どうりで）ウワンダァ
- ☐ Close!（惜しい！）クロウス
- ☐ Me, too.（私もだよ）
- ☐ Me, either. / Me, neither.（私も〜ないよ）イーザァ ニーザァ
- ☐ That's right. / Exactly!（そのとおり）イグゼァクトリィ

● うれしい

- ☐ I did it! / Yes!（やったぁ！）
- ☐ Bingo!（当ったりー！）
- ☐ I'm so touched!（感激！）タチュト

● 驚く

- ☐ Oh, my goodness! / Gosh!（うへー！ げげっ！）グドネィス ガシュ
- ☐ Unbelievable!（信じられない！）アンビリーヴァブゥ
- ☐ No kidding.（まさか）キディング
- ☐ No way!（ありえない）

● 怒る

- ☐ I can't stand it!（もう我慢できない）
- ☐ I'm angry.（頭に来た）エアングゥリィ
- ☐ That's enough.（イナフ）
- ☐ Give me a break.（いいかげんにして）ブレイゥ

● 謝るとき

- ☐ I'm sorry. / Sorry.（ごめんなさい）
- ☐ I'm really sorry. / I'm terribly sorry.（本当にごめんなさい）テゥラブリィ

● 気にしないで

- ☐ That's all right. / No problem.（いいよ，いいよ）プラブラム
- ☐ Don't worry about it.（気にしないで）

★他にもこんな言い方があるよ！

- ☐ Why? / How come?（どうして？）
- ☐ I told you.（言っただろ！）
- ☐ Here you are. / Here it is.（はい，どうぞ）
- ☐ After you. / You go first. / Go ahead.（お先にどうぞ）
- ☐ I don't care. / It doesn't matter.（かまいませんよ）メアタァ
- ☐ Come on.（さあ！）
- ☐ It's up to you. / You can decide.（君次第だよ）ディサイド
- ☐ I'll do it. / Leave it to me.（私に任せて）リーヴ
- ☐ It's none of your business.（余計なお世話だよ）ナンヌ ビズネィス
- ☐ Leave me alone.（放っておいてよ）アロウンヌ

先生や友だちの言ったことに対して，英語であいづちを打ったり自分の感じたことを言ったりしてみよう！

● 励ます

☐ Don't worry. / Don't be afraid.
アフゥレイド
（心配しないで）

☐ Take it easy.
（気楽にいこうよ）

☐ Go for it! / Do your best.
（がんばれ）

☐ Good luck. （幸運を祈ります）
☐ That's too bad. （お気の毒に）
☐ It can't be helped. （しかたないよ）
☐ Never mind. （気にするな）
☐ Forget it. （忘れなよ）

● ほめる

☐ Good for you.
（よかったね）

☐ Good idea. (いい考えだね)
☐ Great! / Excellent! / Cool!
エクサラント
（すごいね！）

● 注意を促すとき

☐ Be careful! / Watch out!
（気をつけて！　危ない！）

☐ Stop it! （やめてよ）
☐ Be quiet. （静かに）
☐ Calm down. （落ち着いて）
カーム
☐ Be serious. （真剣にやって）
スィァゥリァス

● 相手の考えを聞く

☐ How about you?
（あなたはどうですか？）

☐ What do you think?
（君はどう思う？）

● ありがとう

☐ Thank you. （ありがとう）
☐ Thanks. / Thanks a lot. （どうも）
☐ Thank you so much. / Thank you very much.
（大変ありがとうございます）

● どういたしまして

☐ You're welcome.
☐ Not at all. / Don't mention it. / It's my pleasure.
メンシュンヌ
プレジュァ
（どういたしまして）

☐ Have it your way! （勝手にしたら！）
☐ It's no big deal. （大したことじゃないよ）
ディーゥ
☐ That's not fair! （ずるいよ）
フェア
☐ It's a pity. / What a shame! （残念！）
ピティ　シュエイム
☐ I mean it. （本気です）
☐ What do you mean? （どういう意味？）
☐ It's a secret. （内緒です）
☐ Trust me! （信じてよ）
チュアスト
☐ Gross! （気持ち悪い！）
グゥロウス
☐ What a pain! （面倒くさいなぁ！）
ペインス
☐ I didn't mean it. （そんなつもりじゃなかったんです）

Let's Start 3

Classroom English
いろいろな場面で使える便利な表現 2

★あいさつ

●やあ！

- [ ] Hi, there.（やあ！）
- [ ] Long time no see.
  （お久しぶり）

●おめでとう
- [ ] Congratulations!（おめでとう）
  （カングゥレアチュレイシュンズ）
- [ ] Happy birthday, Ken.
  （お誕生日おめでとう，ケン）
- [ ] Merry Christmas!
  （メリークリスマス！）
- [ ] Happy New Year!
  （新年おめでとうございます）

●じゃあ，またね
- [ ] Good-bye. / Bye-bye. /
  Bye for now.（さようなら）
- [ ] See you.（じゃあ，またね）
- [ ] See you later.（また後で）
  （レイタァ）
- [ ] See you next Monday.
  （また来週の月曜日に）
- [ ] Have a nice day [weekend]!
  （ウィーケンド）
  （よい日[週末]を）

●ごきげんいかが？

- [ ] How are you (doing)?

●どうしたの？

- [ ] What's the matter?
  （メアタァ）
- [ ] What's wrong?
  （ゥローング）
  （どうしたの？）
- [ ] That's too bad.
- [ ] I'm very sorry to hear
  that.（お気の毒に）
- [ ] Take care.（お大事に）
  （ケア）

●今の気分・調子は…

- [ ] Great!（絶好調！） - [ ] I'm fine.（元気） - [ ] I'm OK.（普通）
  （グゥレイト）

- [ ] So-so.（まあまあ） - [ ] I don't feel well. - [ ] Terrible.（最悪）
  （気分が悪い） （テゥラブゥ）

- [ ] I'm hungry. - [ ] I'm sleepy. - [ ] I'm tired.
  （ハングリィ） （眠い） （タイアド）
  （お腹がすいている） （疲れたよ）

- [ ] Not too bad.（そんなに悪くないよ）
- [ ] Not so good.（あまり良くない）
- [ ] I'm hot [cold]!（暑い[寒い]！）
- [ ] I'm thirsty.（のどが乾いた）
  （スアースティ）
- [ ] I have a cold [fever / sore throat].
  （フィーヴァ　ソー　スゥロウト）
  （風邪をひいている[熱がある／のどが痛い]）

Let's Start

★ 依頼する

☐ Will [Can] you 〜？（〜してくれませんか？）

（例）Will you lend me your red pen?
　　　（赤ペンを貸してくれませんか？）
　　　Can you open the window?
　　　（窓を開けてくれませんか？）
　　　Will you do me a favor?（フェイヴァ）（お願いがあります）
　　　※Would [Could] you 〜?（ゥヂュ ｸﾞﾁｭ）と言うと、より丁寧になるよ！

★ 許可する

☐ Can [May] I 〜？（〜してもいいですか？）

（例）May I speak in Japanese?
　　　（日本語で話してもいいですか？）
　　　Can I borrow your eraser?（バゥロゥ イゥレイサァ）
　　　（消しゴムを借りてもいい？）

★ 誘う

☐ Shall we 〜？（シェアゥ）（〜しませんか？）

（例）Shall we go shopping together?（タゲザァ）
　　　（いっしょに買い物に行きませんか？）

☐ Let's 〜．（〜しましょう）

（例）Let's play tennis after school.
　　　（放課後テニスをしようよ）

★ すすめる

☐ How about 〜？（〜はいかが？）

（例）How about a cookie?（クッキーはいかが？）

☐ Why don't you 〜？（〜しない？）

（例）Why don't you join us?（ごいっしょしませんか？）

☐ Why not?（そうしてみましょうよ）

★ 申し出る

☐ Shall I 〜？（〜しましょうか？）

（例）Shall I open the window?（窓を開けましょうか？）

● いいよ！

☐ OK.　　　　☐ Sure.（サートンリィ）
☐ Certainly.　☐ Yes, of course.
☐ All right.　☐ Go ahead.（アヘド）

● 悪いけれど…

☐ Sorry, but 〜

（例）Sorry, but I'm busy now.
　　　（悪いけれど、今忙しいんだ）

☐ No, I'm afraid you can't.（アフゥレイド）
　　　（残念ながら、できません）

☐ No way.（冗談じゃないよ）

　　　※断るときは、理由を加えましょう。

● 誘い・すすめに答える

☐ Yes. That's a good idea.
☐ That's great.（グゥレイト）（そりゃあいい）
☐ I'd love to.（喜んで）
☐ That sounds interesting [like fun].（サゥンヅ インタゥレスティング）（面白そう）
☐ I'm sorry, I can't.
　　　（残念ですが、できません）
☐ No, thank you.
　　　（ありがとう。でもダメなの）
☐ No, let's not.（だめなんだ）

● 申し出に答える

☐ Yes, please.（お願い）
☐ No, thank you.（結構です）
☐ No, you don't have to.（ヘァフタ）
　　　（しなくていいよ）

Topic 1

家について話そう！
In the House

- ① gate 門
- ② front door 入り口
- ③ nameplate 表札
- ④ window 窓
- ⑤ shutter シャッター
- ⑥ roof 屋根
- ⑦ fence へい
- ⑧ chimney えんとつ
- ⑨ shed 物置
- ⑩ balcony ベランダ
- ⑪ garage 車庫
- ⑫ shoe closet 下駄箱
- ⑬ floor 床
- ⑭ ceiling 天井
- ⑮ stairs 階段
- ⑯ living room 居間
- ⑰ bookcase 本棚
- ⑱ sofa ソファ
- ⑲ heater ストーブ
- ⑳ fan 扇風機
- ㉑ air conditioner エアコン
- ㉒ light 明かり
- ㉓ carpet カーペット
- ㉔ TV [television] テレビ
- ㉕ stereo ステレオ
- ㉖ telephone 電話
- ㉗ bedroom 寝室
- ㉘ chest of drawers 洋服だんす
- ㉙ closet 押入れ
- ㉚ pillow 枕
- ㉛ alarm clock 目覚まし時計
- ㉜ vacuum cleaner 掃除機
- ㉝ broom ほうき
- ㉞ feather duster はたき
- ㉟ dustpan ちりとり
- ㊱ dresser 鏡台
- ㊲ nail clippers 爪切り
- ㊳ ear pick 耳かき
- ㊴ bed ベッド
- ㊵ quilt かけ布団
- ㊶ futon しき布団
- ㊷ blanket 毛布

Part 1

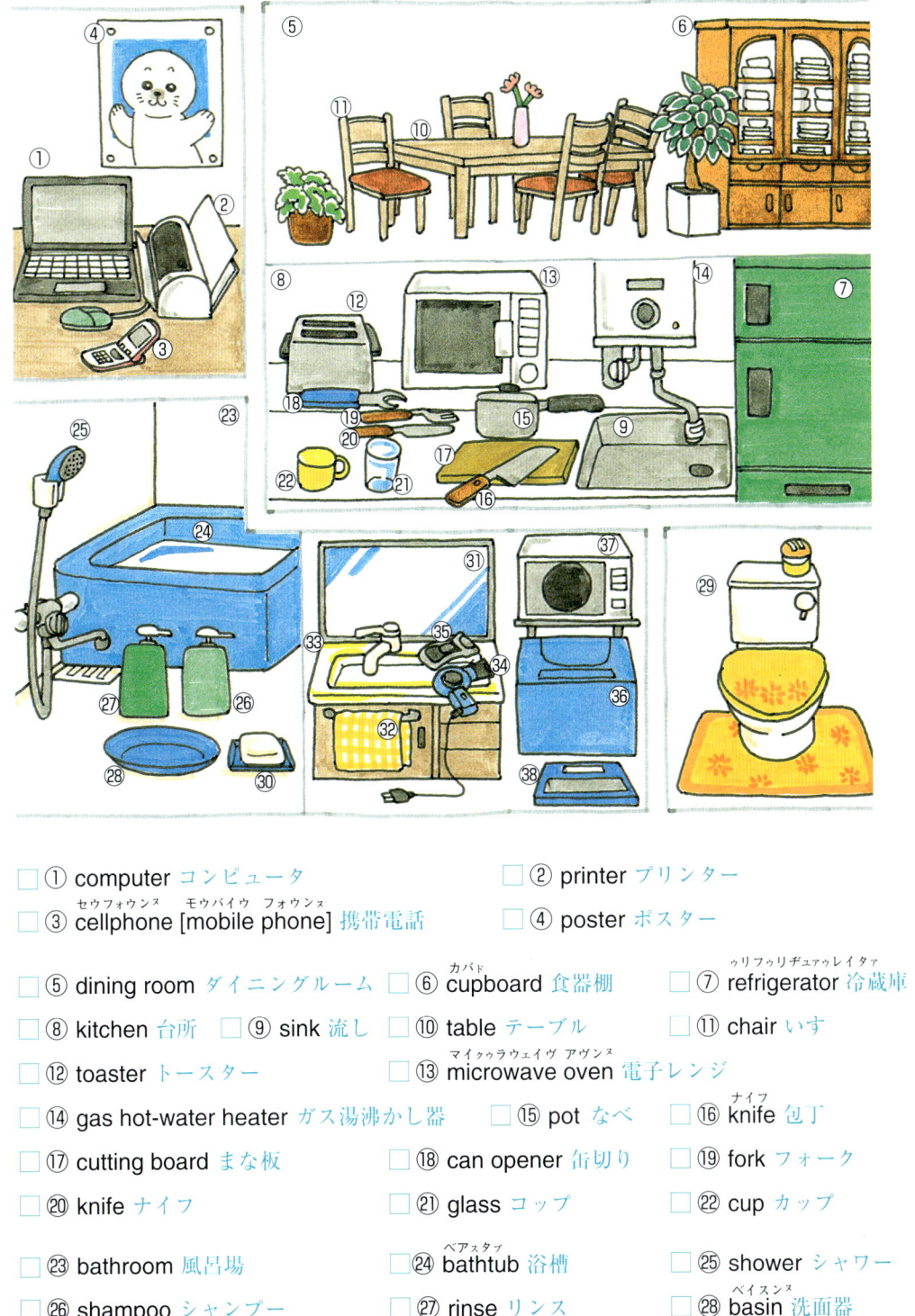

- ① computer コンピュータ
- ② printer プリンター
- ③ cellphone [mobile phone] 携帯電話
- ④ poster ポスター
- ⑤ dining room ダイニングルーム
- ⑥ cupboard 食器棚
- ⑦ refrigerator 冷蔵庫
- ⑧ kitchen 台所
- ⑨ sink 流し
- ⑩ table テーブル
- ⑪ chair いす
- ⑫ toaster トースター
- ⑬ microwave oven 電子レンジ
- ⑭ gas hot-water heater ガス湯沸かし器
- ⑮ pot なべ
- ⑯ knife 包丁
- ⑰ cutting board まな板
- ⑱ can opener 缶切り
- ⑲ fork フォーク
- ⑳ knife ナイフ
- ㉑ glass コップ
- ㉒ cup カップ
- ㉓ bathroom 風呂場
- ㉔ bathtub 浴槽
- ㉕ shower シャワー
- ㉖ shampoo シャンプー
- ㉗ rinse リンス
- ㉘ basin 洗面器
- ㉙ toilet トイレ
- ㉚ soap 石けん
- ㉛ mirror 鏡
- ㉜ towel タオル
- ㉝ washstand 洗面台
- ㉞ dryer ドライヤー
- ㉟ shaver ひげそり
- ㊱ washing machine 洗濯機
- ㊲ electric dryer 乾燥機
- ㊳ scale 体重計

9

Topic 2 まちについて話そう！
In Your Town

- ① drugstore 薬局
- ② bakery パン屋
- ③ restaurant レストラン
- ④ theater 映画館・劇場
- ⑤ toy store おもちゃ屋
- ⑥ flower shop 花屋
- ⑦ department store デパート
- ⑧ grocery store 食料品店
- ⑨ convenience store コンビニ
- ⑩ factory 工場
- ⑪ gas station ガソリンスタンド
- ⑫ amusement park 遊園地
- ⑬ baseball stadium [ballpark] 野球場
- ⑭ park 公園
- ⑮ museum 博物館
- ⑯ art museum 美術館
- ⑰ police station 警察署
- ⑱ police box 交番
- ⑲ fire station 消防署
- ⑳ city hall 市役所
- ㉑ bank 銀行
- ㉒ school 学校
- ㉓ hospital 病院
- ㉔ post office 郵便局
- ㉕ office building 会社
- ㉖ parking lot 駐車場
- ㉗ pay phone 公衆電話
- ㉘ public lavatory 公衆トイレ
- ㉙ vending machine 自動販売機

Part 1

- ① apartment house アパート
- ② condo [condominium] マンション
- ③ station 駅
- ④ subway [underground] 地下鉄
- ⑤ railroad 鉄道
- ⑥ train 列車
- ⑦ bus バス
- ⑧ bus stop バス停
- ⑨ timetable 時刻表
- ⑩ fare chart 運賃表
- ⑪ ticket window 切符売り場
- ⑫ ticket gate 改札口
- ⑬ highway 幹線道路
- ⑭ expressway 高速道路
- ⑮ intersection 交差点
- ⑯ crosswalk 横断歩道
- ⑰ street 通り
- ⑱ traffic light 信号機
- ⑲ mountain 山
- ⑳ forest 森
- ㉑ woods 林
- ㉒ hill 丘
- ㉓ farm 農園
- ㉔ lake 湖
- ㉕ river 川
- ㉖ boat ボート
- ㉗ ship 船
- ㉘ bank 堤防
- ㉙ rice field 田んぼ
- ㉚ pond 池
- ㉛ bridge 橋
- ㉜ orchard 果樹園
- ㉝ playground 運動場
- ㉞ temple 寺
- ㉟ shrine 神社
- ㊱ valley 谷
- ㊲ village 村
- ㊳ sea 海
- ㊴ beach 海岸
- ㊵ sky 空
- ㊶ rainbow 虹
- ㊷ cloud 雲
- ㊸ sun 太陽
- ㊹ road 道路

11

Topic 3

自分のことについて話そう！
Let's Talk about Ourselves!

● Model Dialogue ●

A: What's your hobby?
B: I like making models. How about you?
A: I like skiing very much. I go skiing four or five times every winter. Do you ski?
B: No, I don't.
A: What sports do you like?
B: I like swimming. I go swimming at the beach every summer. I like summer better than winter.

A: 趣味は何？
B: 模型作りかな。君は？
A: スキーが大好きなの。一冬に４，５回はスキーに行くかな。あなたはスキーするの？
B: しないけど。
A: どんなスポーツが好きなの？
B: 水泳だよ。毎年夏は，海に泳ぎに行くんだ。だから冬より夏が好きなんだ。

趣味は次の表現を使って言えるよ！
・enjoy ～ing.（私は～をして楽しみます）
・My hobby is ～ing.（私の趣味は～することです）
・I like ～ ing.（私は～するのが好きです）

☐ watching TV
（テレビを見る）

☐ playing soccer
（サッカーをする）

☐ playing the piano
（ピアノを弾く）

☐ reading books
（読書）

☐ cooking
（料理）

☐ painting
（絵画）

☐ fishing
（つり）

☐ knitting (ネィティング)
（編み物）

☐ listening to music
（音楽鑑賞）

☐ watching movies
（映画鑑賞）

☐ collecting stamps (カレクティング)
（切手収集）

☐ hiking up mountains (ハイキング)
（登山）

☐ traveling
（旅行）

Part 1

○話題を広げよう！

<例1>自分自身の話→好きなスポーツの話→将来の夢の話　　➡ Topic 11参照。
<例2>自分自身の話→ファッションの話→買い物の話　　　➡ Topic 6，Topic 15参照。

★ Words & Phrases ★

- □ 私の好きな〜 My favorite 〜（フェイヴァリット）
- □ 〜に夢中です be crazy about 〜．（クレイズィ）
- □ 〜したい want to 〜．
- □ 長所 good point
- □ 短所 weak point
- □ 血液型 blood type（ブラド）
- □ （商業／工業／農業）高校 (commercial / technical / agricultural) high school（カマーシャウ／テクネィカウ／エアグゥリカウチュアウ）
- □ 公立[私立]高校 public [private] high school（プブリヴィト）
- □ 性格 personality（パーサネアリティ）　➡ 付録1 参照。

〈趣味：hobbies〉

- □ 小説 novel（ナヴァウ）
- □ 古典 classics（クレアスィクス）
- □ ＳＦ science fiction（サイエンス フィクシュンス）
- □ マンガ comics
- □ 雑誌 magazine
- □ 推理小説 detective story（ディテクティヴ）
- □ ミステリー mystery（ミスタゥリィ）
- □ マンガを描くこと drawing cartoons（カートゥーンスス）
- □ （楽器）を演奏する play the 〜
- □ カラオケ karaoke
- □ ポップス pops
- □ クラシック classical music（クレアスィカウ）
- □ ジャズ jazz
- □ ロック rock
- □ ライヴ live concert
- □ 買い物 shopping
- □ 買い物に行く go shopping
- □ ウインドーショッピング window-shopping
- □ お菓子を作る make cakes
- □ お笑い comedy（カミディ）
- □ 〜収集 collecting 〜
- □ 〜を集める collect 〜
- □ テレビゲームをする play a video game
- □ レンタルビデオを見る watch a rental video
- □ 踊り dancing
- □ キャンプ camping
- □ サーフィン surfing
- □ ジョギング jogging
- □ 水上スキー water-skiing
- □ ヨット sailboat
- □ ハイキング hiking
- □ 100m泳ぐ swim 100m
- □ フリスビー Frisbee
- □ 〜へ日帰り旅行する take [make] a day trip to 〜
- □ 1日おきに every other day
- □ 1週間に1[2／3]回 once [twice / three times] a week
- □ ほとんど毎日 almost every day

★ Expressions in Use ★

- ・Let me introduce myself.（自己紹介をさせてください。）
- ・I'm in the first [second / third] year of junior high school.（中学1[2／3]年生です）
- ・I'm from Saitama.（私は埼玉県出身です）
- ・I'm on the baseball team. [I belong to the baseball team.]（ビローング）（私は野球部です）　➡ Topic 11 参照。
- ・I want to be a fire fighter.（ファイア ファイタァ）（私は消防士になりたい）　➡ Topic 4 参照。
- ・I'm (not) good at cooking.（私は料理が(不)得意です）
- ・I'm interested in Major League Baseball.（メイヂュア リーグ）（私はメジャーリーグに興味がある）
- ・I can do a back flip.（フリプ）（私はバク転をすることができる）
- ・My blood type is A.（私の血液型はA型です）
- ・My sign of the zodiac is 〜．（サインス ゾウディエアク）（私の星座は〜です）

  - 牡羊座 Aries（エァリーズ）
  - 牡牛座 Taurus（トーラス）
  - 双子座 Gemini（ヂュエミナイ）
  - かに座 Cancer（ケアンサァ）
  - しし座 Leo（リーオウ）
  - 乙女座 Virgo（ヴァーゴウ）
  - 天秤座 Libra（リーブラァ）
  - さそり座 Scorpio（スコーピオウ）
  - 射手座 Sagittarius（セアヂュァテァリゥス）
  - 山羊座 Capricorn（ケアプリコーン）
  - 水瓶座 Aquarius（アクウェアリゥス）
  - 魚座 Pisces（パイスィーズ）

- ・I have been to Hawaii.（私はハワイへ行ったことがある）

Topic 4

家族のことについて話そう！
Let's Talk about Our Families!

● **Model Dialogue** ●

A: How many people are there in your family?
B: Four. I have an older brother. How about you?
A: I have five people in my family. I have a sister and my grandmother lives with us.
B: How old is your grandmother?
A: She is seventy-five years old. She is really healthy. She goes for a walk to the park every day.

A: 何人家族？
B: 4人だよ。兄が1人いるんだ。君の家族は何人？
A: 5人だよ。妹とおばあちゃんといっしょに住んでいるんだ。
B: おばあちゃんは何歳？
A: 75歳だよ。とっても元気なんだ。毎日公園まで散歩に行くよ。

☐ father（父）　　　　　　　☐ mother（母）
☐ older [big] brother（兄）　☐ older [big] sister（姉）
☐ younger [little] brother（弟）☐ younger [little] sister（妹）
☐ grandfather（祖父）　　　☐ grandmother（祖母）

○話題を広げよう！

<例1>兄弟姉妹の話→彼[彼女]が得意なスポーツの話→将来の職業の話
<例2>祖母の話→料理が好きだという話→お正月におせちを作ってくれるという話

★ Words & Phrases ★

- □ いとこ (カズンヌ) cousin
- □ おい (ネフュー) nephew
- □ おじさん (アンクゥ) uncle
- □ 夫 (ハズバンド) husband
- □ おばさん (エアント) aunt
- □ 義理の兄[姉] brother [sister]-in-law (ロー)
- □ 親戚 (ゥレラティヴ) relative
- □ 妻 wife
- □ はとこ second cousin (セカンド)
- □ ひいおじいちゃん great-grandfather
- □ ひいおばあちゃん great-grandmother
- □ ペット pet
- □ 孫 grandchild [grandchildren / grandson / granddaughter] (グゥレアンドチュアイゥド)
- □ めい (ニース) niece
- □ 両親 (ペァランツ) parents
- □ 同い年のいとこ cousin of my age
- □ 長男 oldest [eldest] son (エゥディスト)
- □ 長女 oldest [eldest] daughter (ドータァ)
- □ 二[三]男 second [third] son
- □ 二[三]女 second [third] daughter
- □ 末っ子 youngest child
- □ 高校生 high school student
- □ 大学生 college [university] student
- □ 専門学校生 vocational college student (ヴォウケイシァヌゥ カリヂュ)
- □ 浪人生 student who failed his [her] (フェイゥド) college entrance examinations and is studying to take them again (エンチュァンス イッゼアミネイシュンズ)
- □ 単身赴任者 a person who lives away from his [her] family because of his [her] job

〈職業 occupations〉

- □ アナウンサー announcer
- □ 医者 doctor
- □ イラストレーター illustrator
- □ 映画監督 film director
- □ 音楽家 musician
- □ 外交官 diplomat (ディプラメアト)
- □ 会社員 office clerk
- □ 画家 artist / painter
- □ 科学者 scientist (サイァンティスト)
- □ 看護師 nurse
- □ 技師 engineer (エンヂュイニァ)
- □ 教師 teacher
- □ 漁業従事者 fisherman
- □ 警察官 police officer
- □ 建築家 architect (アーキテクト)
- □ 公務員 public official (アゥイシュゥ)
- □ コンピュータプログラマー computer programmer
- □ 裁判官 judge
- □ 作家 writer
- □ 作曲家 composer (カムポウザァ)
- □ サラリーマン salaried worker
- □ 自動車工 auto mechanic (オートゥ ミケアネィク)
- □ 写真家 photographer (ファタグゥラファ)
- □ 獣医 vet (ヴェト)
- □ 小説家 novelist (ナヴァリスト)
- □ 消防士 fire fighter
- □ 新聞記者 newspaper reporter
- □ 政治家 politician (パリティシュンヌ)
- □ 専業主婦 full-time homemaker
- □ 僧侶 priest (プゥリースト)
- □ 大工 carpenter
- □ 通訳 interpreter (インターブリタァ)
- □ デザイナー designer
- □ テレビプロデューサー TV producer
- □ 店主 storekeeper
- □ 添乗員 tour conductor
- □ ニュースキャスター newscaster
- □ 庭師 gardener (ガードナァ)
- □ 農業従事者 farmer
- □ 歯医者 dentist (デンティスト)
- □ 俳優[女優] actor [actress]
- □ 花屋さん florist (フロゥリスト)
- □ 美容師 beautician (ビューティシュンヌ)
- □ プロの〜 professional 〜
- □ 弁護士 lawyer (ローヤァ)
- □ 翻訳家 translator (チュエアンスレイタァ)
- □ 漫画家 cartoonist (カートゥーニスト)
- □ 薬剤師 pharmacist (ファーマスィスト)
- □ 幼稚園の先生 kindergarten teacher (キンダガートン)
- □ 理容師 barber
- □ 料理人 chef / cook
- □ 旅客乗務員 flight attendant (アテンダント)

★ Expressions in Use ★

- I have five people in my family. [There're five people in my family.] （うちは5人家族です）
- My brother is three years older [younger] than I [me]. （私の兄[弟]は3歳年上[下]です）
- I often have a quarrel with my brother [sister]. （よく兄弟げんかをする） (クウォ(一)ゥラウ)
- I take care of my brother. （弟の面倒を見る）
- My grandmother gives me pocket money. （おばあちゃんからお小遣いをもらう）
- I live in an apartment [a condo]. （マンションに住んでいる）

Topic 5 朝起きてから寝るまで
Daily Routines

● **Model Dialogue** ●

A: What time do you usually get up?
B: I usually get up at five thirty.
A: Five thirty? Why do you get up so early?
B: Because I do my homework, study, and read books.
A: So what time do you usually go to bed?
B: At nine o'clock.
A: Wow. I usually go to bed around one.
B: Really? What time do you usually get up?
A: At eight.

A: いつも何時に起きるの？
B: いつもは5時半かな。
A: 5時半？ なんでそんなに早いの？
B: なんでって，宿題したり，勉強したり本を読んだりしてるから。
A: じゃ，何時に寝てるの？
B: 9時だよ。
A: えぇ！ ぼくはいつも1時ごろだよ。
B: 本当？ いつも何時に起きるの？
A: 8時だよ。

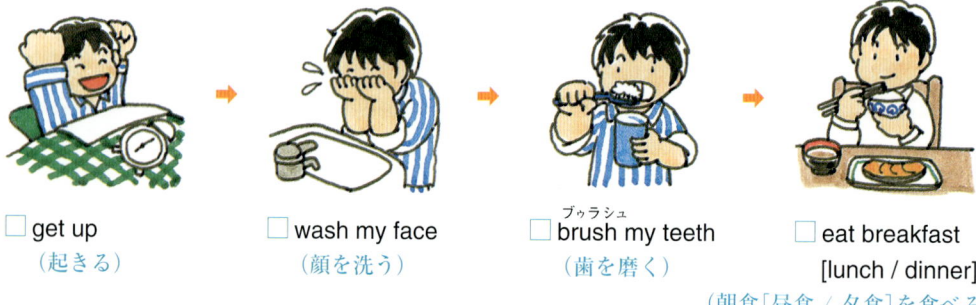

☐ get up （起きる）
☐ wash my face （顔を洗う）
☐ brush my teeth ブラシュ （歯を磨く）
☐ eat breakfast [lunch / dinner] （朝食[昼食／夕食]を食べる）

☐ go to bed （寝る）
☐ take a bath （風呂に入る）
☐ watch TV （テレビを見る）
☐ do my homework （宿題をする）
☐ go to school （学校へ行く）

○話題を広げよう！

<例1>早起きするという話→朝食を自分で用意するという話→好きな食べ物の話
<例2>夜更かしの話→居眠りの話→先生に怒られた話

★ Words & Phrases ★ → Topic 3，Topic 7 参照。

〈朝起きてから学校へ行くまで〉

- ☐ 目覚し時計を止める［セットする］ turn off ［set］ the alarm clock
- ☐ 髪をとかす comb my hair
- ☐ トイレに行く go to the bathroom
- ☐ （衣服を）着る put on ～
- ☐ 洗濯物を干す hang the laundry out to dry
- ☐ 靴を履く［脱ぐ］ put on ［take off］ my shoes
- ☐ 傘を持っていく take an umbrella with me
- ☐ 家を出る leave my house
- ☐ 自転車で学校へ行く go to school by bike
- ☐ 自転車に鍵をかける lock my bike
- ☐ 歩いて学校へ行く walk to school
- ☐ 交差点［横断歩道］を渡る cross the street at the intersection ［pedestrian crossing］
- ☐ 電車に乗る（降りる） get on ［off］ the train
- ☐ ～に席をゆずる give my seat to ～
- ☐ 学校に着く arrive at school
- ☐ 学校に遅刻する be late for school

〈学校〉

- ☐ あいさつを交わす say hello to each other
- ☐ 一生懸命勉強する study hard
- ☐ 給食を食べる eat the school lunch
- ☐ 図書室［館］に行く go to the library
- ☐ 教室の掃除をする clean our classroom
- ☐ 体育館でバスケットボールをする play basketball in the gym
- ☐ 友だちとおしゃべりをする chat with my friends
- ☐ 本屋へ立ち寄る drop in at the bookstore

〈学校から帰宅してから〉

- ☐ 帰宅する get home
- ☐ 着替える change my clothes
- ☐ ヘッドホンで音楽を聞く listen to music on my headphones
- ☐ ボリュームを上げる［下げる］ turn up ［down］ the volume
- ☐ うたた寝をする take a nap
- ☐ 寝転がる lie down
- ☐ 犬を散歩に連れていく take my dog for a walk
- ☐ おやつを食べる have a snack
- ☐ うがいをする gargle
- ☐ 洗濯物を取り込む take in the laundry
- ☐ 猫にえさをやる feed my cat
- ☐ 犬の世話をする take care of my dog
- ☐ 買い物に行く go shopping
- ☐ ～を買う buy ～
- ☐ マフラーを編む knit a scarf ［muffler］
- ☐ お茶［コーヒー］を入れる make tea ［coffee］
- ☐ テーブルを片付ける clean the table
- ☐ 友だちに電話する call my friend
- ☐ 友だちと電話で話す talk with my friend on the phone
- ☐ 音楽を聴く listen to music
- ☐ 読書する read a book
- ☐ トランプをする play cards
- ☐ あやとりをする play cat's cradle
- ☐ チェスをする play chess
- ☐ パソコンゲームをする play a computer game
- ☐ 部屋の掃除をする clean my room
- ☐ ～を乾かす dry ～
- ☐ 布団をしく spread out my *futon*
- ☐ 風呂に入る take a bath
- ☐ シャワーを浴びる take a shower
- ☐ ～を迎えに行く go to meet ～
- ☐ 薬を飲む take medicine
- ☐ 寝る go to bed

Topic 6: 芸能・ファッションについて話そう！
Let's Talk about Entertainment and Fashion!

● Model Dialogue ●

A: What kind of clothes do you like?
B: I like Ayumi Hamasaki's clothes. I often wear clothes like hers.
A: So you like flashy ones. Your skirt's nice. Where do you usually go shopping for clothes?
B: Well, I have some favorite shops in the city. And I sometimes go to some stores in Harajuku.
A: Really? I've never been there.
B: Would you like to go there with me this Sunday?
A: Great! I'd like to buy a new sweater.

A: どんな洋服が好きなの？
B: 浜崎あゆみが好きでね，彼女のような洋服をよく着ているかな。
A: じゃ，けっこう派手めの物が好きなのね。かわいいスカートね。洋服はだいたいどこで買っているの？
B: 街に気に入ったお店があるし，時には原宿にも出かけていくわ。
A: うそ？ 私一度も行ったことないのよ。
B: じゃ，今度の日曜日にいっしょに行かない？
A: 本当！ ちょうど新しいセーターでも買いたいと思っていたところよ。

☐ singer（歌手）　☐ musician（音楽家）　☐ actor/actress（俳優）　☐ newscaster（キャスター）　☐ reporter（レポーター）

☐ ring（指輪）
☐ sneakers（スニーカー）
☐ beard（あごひげ）
☐ mustache（口ひげ）
☐ skirt（スカート）
☐ tie（ネクタイ）

☐ sweater（セーター）
☐ jacket（ジャケット）
☐ T-shirt（Tシャツ）
☐ dress（ワンピース）
☐ shoes（くつ）
☐ glasses（メガネ）

☐ jeans（ジーンズ）
☐ vest（ベスト）
☐ shorts（半ズボン）
☐ coat（コート）
☐ shirt（シャツ）

○話題を広げよう！
＜例1＞自分の特技の話→好きなテレビ番組の話→憧れの職業の話　➡ Topic 3 参照。
＜例2＞好きな芸能人の話→好きなファッションの話→買い物の話　➡ Topic 15 参照。

★ Words & Phrases ★

〈洋服 clothes〉
- ☐ イヤリング earrings
- ☐ カーディガン cardigan
- ☐ キャミソール camisole top
- ☐ 靴下 socks
- ☐ 毛皮のコート fur coat
- ☐ サンダル sandals
- ☐ 下着 underwear
- ☐ スカーフ scarf
- ☐ ストッキング pantyhose
- ☐ ズボン trousers / pants
- ☐ 制服 school uniform
- ☐ タートルネック turtleneck
- ☐ タンクトップ tank top
- ☐ 手袋 gloves
- ☐ 手袋（親指以外は分かれていない）mittens
- ☐ トレーナー sweat shirt
- ☐ 長そでの〜 long-sleeved 〜
- ☐ ネックレス necklace
- ☐ ノースリーブの〜 sleeveless 〜
- ☐ ハイヒール high heels
- ☐ ハンカチ handkerchief
- ☐ 半そでの〜 short-sleeved 〜
- ☐ ピアス pierced earrings
- ☐ Vネック V-neck
- ☐ ブーツ high boots
- ☐ フード付きの〜 hooded 〜
- ☐ ブラジャー bra
- ☐ ブレザー blazer
- ☐ ベルト belt
- ☐ ポケット pocket
- ☐ ボタン button
- ☐ マフラー scarf [muffler]
- ☐ 丸首 round-neck
- ☐ ミニスカート miniskirt

〈ヘアスタイル hairstyles〉
- ☐ おかっぱ pageboy style
- ☐ 髪を切る have a haircut
- ☐ くせ毛 (naturally) curly hair
- ☐ ストレートヘア straight hair
- ☐ 茶髪（染めた）dyed hair
- ☐ ポニーテール ponytail
- ☐ 前髪 bangs
- ☐ 三つ編み braids
- ☐ パーマをかける have my hair permed
- ☐ 結ぶ，結う tie

〈ファッション fashion〉
- ☐ いかした funky
- ☐ カジュアルな casual
- ☐ かっこいい cool
- ☐ かわいい cute
- ☐ ゴージャスな gorgeous
- ☐ 最新の the latest
- ☐ 地味な plain
- ☐ ダサい out of style
- ☐ 伝統的な traditional
- ☐ 70年代ファッション seventies fashion
- ☐ 派手な flashy

〈芸能 entertainment〉
- ☐ アイドル歌手 pop idol
- ☐ 映画 movie / film / cinema
- ☐ 映画館 movie theater
- ☐ 映画スター movie star
- ☐ お笑い芸人 comedian
- ☐ 外国映画 foreign movie
- ☐ 記事 story / article
- ☐ クイズ番組 quiz show
- ☐ 芸能界 the entertainment world
- ☐ 芸能人 entertainer
- ☐ ゴールデンタイム prime time
- ☐ コンサート concert
- ☐ サスペンス mystery story
- ☐ 主人公 hero / heroine
- ☐ 深夜番組 late program
- ☐ チャンネル channel
- ☐ テレビ局 TV station
- ☐ トーク番組 talk show
- ☐ ドキュメンタリー documentary
- ☐ ニュース番組 news broadcast
- ☐ バラエティー番組 variety show
- ☐ バラード ballad
- ☐ バンド (rock) band
- ☐ ヒップホップ hip-hop
- ☐ 冒険映画 adventure movie
- ☐ マスコミ mass media
- ☐ ミュージカル musical
- ☐ ライブ live (concerts)
- ☐ ラップ rap
- ☐ ラブストーリー love story
- ☐ 連続ドラマ serial drama
- ☐ 脇役 supporting actor

★ Expressions in Use ★

- ・その上着は彼によく似合う。The jacket looks good on him.
- ・私は髪を短く切ってもらった。I had my hair cut short.
- ・ギャグがうけた。（ギャグを外した。）The gag got a big reaction. (The gag bombed.)
- ・私は映画「タイタニック」に感動した。I was moved by the movie *Titanic*.

Topic 7

食事や料理について話そう！
What Would You Like for Breakfast?

● **Model Dialogue** ●

A: We're going to cook something for Nanako on her birthday. I'm going to make spaghetti and potato salad. Will you join us?

B: Of course. By the way, Nanako's favorite is spaghetti with seafood in tomato sauce.

A: I see. I'll try making that one then.

A: 奈名子の誕生日にみんなで何か料理をしようと思っているの。私はスパゲッティとポテトサラダを作るつもりなんだけど、いっしょにやらない？

B: もちろん。そう言えば、奈名子はトマトソースベースのシーフードスパゲッティがお気に入りよ。

A: そう。じゃ，挑戦してみようかな。

☐ breakfast（朝食）

☐ lunch（昼食）

☐ snack（おやつ）

☐ dinner [supper]（夕食）

☐ late-night snack（夜食）

☐ Please help yourself.
[Please have some.]
（どうぞ召し上がれ）

☐ How is it?
[Is everything all right?]
（いかがですか？）

☐ A: Did you have enough?
（お腹いっぱいになりましたか？）
☐ B: Yes, I'm full.
（はい，お腹がいっぱいです）

○話題を広げよう！

＜例1＞料理が好き→帰宅後に買い物に行って料理をする→家族の好きなメニュー
＜例2＞テレビのグルメ番組を見る→外食する→家でまねて作ってみる

★ Words & Phrases ★   ➡ 付録3 参照。

- ☐ アイスクリーム ice cream
- ☐ お好み焼き Japanese-style pancake with vegetables, meat, and seafood
- ☐ おにぎり rice balls
- ☐ オムレツ omelet
- ☐ カキフライ fried oysters
- ☐ カレー（ライス） curry (and rice)
- ☐ 牛丼 beef bowl
- ☐ きゅうりの酢の物 vinegared cucumbers
- ☐ コーヒー coffee
- ☐ こしょう pepper
- ☐ ご飯 rice
- ☐ ごま油 sesame oil
- ☐ 小麦粉 flour
- ☐ コロッケ croquette
- ☐ 酒 sake
- ☐ 刺身 sashimi
- ☐ 砂糖 sugar
- ☐ サラダ salad
- ☐ 塩 salt
- ☐ シチュー stew
- ☐ ジャム jam
- ☐ しょうゆ soy sauce
- ☐ 酢 vinegar
- ☐ すし sushi
- ☐ ステーキ steak
- ☐ スパゲッティ spaghetti
- ☐ ソース sauce
- ☐ ソーダ soda
- ☐ だし soup [broth]
- ☐ チーズ cheese
- ☐ 茶 tea
- ☐ 天ぷら tempura
- ☐ 唐辛子 red pepper
- ☐ 鶏のからあげ french-fried chicken
- ☐ ドレッシング dressings
- ☐ ～どんぶり～ bowl
- ☐ 鍋料理 hot pot
- ☐ 煮物 stew [steamed food]
- ☐ バター butter
- ☐ パン bread
- ☐ ハンバーガー hamburger
- ☐ ひき肉 grinned meat
- ☐ 豚のしょうが焼き ginger-pork
- ☐ フライドチキン fried chicken
- ☐ マスタード mustard
- ☐ マヨネーズ mayonnaise
- ☐ ミートボール meatballs
- ☐ 水 water
- ☐ 味噌汁 miso soup
- ☐ みりん sweet sake for seasoning
- ☐ 目玉焼き fried eggs
- ☐ 麺類 noodles
- ☐ 焼き魚 broiled [roast] fish
- ☐ 野菜スープ vegetable soup
- ☐ 湯 hot water
- ☐ ゆで卵 hard-boiled egg
- ☐ ヨーグルト yogurt
- ☐ ラーメン ramen [Chinese noodles]
- ☐ わさび wasabi [Japanese horseradish]

- ☐ あっさりした light
- ☐ 甘い sweet
- ☐ おいしい delicious [tasty]
- ☐ 辛い hot [spicy]
- ☐ こくがある full-bodied
- ☐ こってりした heavy
- ☐ しょっぱい salty
- ☐ すっぱい sour
- ☐ 苦い bitter
- ☐ ぱさぱさした dry
- ☐ ぱりぱりした crispy
- ☐ まずい not good

- ☐ いためる fry
- ☐ 皮をむく peel
- ☐ 切る cut
- ☐ ～を加える add ～
- ☐ くんせいにする smoke
- ☐ 凍らせる freeze
- ☐ 塩をふる sprinkle salt
- ☐ すりおろす grate
- ☐ 煮る simmer
- ☐ 混ぜる blend / mix
- ☐ 蒸す steam
- ☐ 焼く barbecue / bake
- ☐ ゆでる broil
- ☐ レンジでチンする microwave

★ Expressions in Use ★

- My brother has a lot of likes and dislikes in food. （弟は食べ物の好き嫌いが多い）
- A: Is this for here or to go?（こちらで召し上がりますか，お持ち帰りですか？）
  B: For here, please. [To go, please.]（ここで食べます［持ち帰ります］）
- A: How would you like your steak done?（ステーキの焼き加減はどのようにいたしますか？）
  B: I'd like it medium-rare, please.（ミディアムレアにしてください）
- It's a little too greasy.（ちょっと脂っこいですね）
- Let's eat out tonight.（今晩は外に食べに行こうよ）

Topic 8

休日・行事や日本文化について話そう！
Holidays, Events, and Japanese Culture

● **Model Dialogue** ●

A: What are your plans for tomorrow?
B: Well, I have nothing special to do.
A: How about going to see a movie with me, then?
B: Fine. Where shall we go?
A: Let's go to Odaiba.
B: What shall we see?
A: How about *The Matrix Revolutions*?
B: Great! What time shall we meet at the station?
A: At eleven in the morning.
B: OK. See you then!

A: 明日の予定は何かある？
B: 特に何もないけれど。
A: じゃ，いっしょに映画でも見に行かない？
B: いいね。どこへ行く？
A: お台場に行こうよ。
B: 何を観ようか？
A: 「マトリックス・レボリューション」はどう？
B: いいねえ！　何時に駅で待ちあわせようか？
A: 午前11時でどうかな？
B: いいよ。じゃあね。

☐ New Year
（新年／お正月）

☐ St. Valentine's Day
（バレンタインデー）

☐ Doll's Festival
（ひな祭り）

エンチュァンス　セゥラモウネィ
☐ entrance ceremony
（入学式）

グゥレアヂュエイシュンス
☐ graduation ceremony
（卒業式）

☐ rainy season
（梅雨）

☐ Star Festival
（七夕）

☐ summer vacation
（夏休み）

☐ Christmas
（クリスマス）

Part 1

○話題を広げよう！

<例1> 冬休みの過ごし方→趣味のスノーボードの話　　➡ Topic 3, 4, 12 参照。
<例2> バレンタインデーの話→友だちの話→自分の話　➡ Topic 3, 12 参照。

★ Words & Phrases ★

〈日本の祝日と年中行事 National Holidays of Japan and Annual Events〉

4月　☐ 始業式 opening ceremony　☐ お花見 cherry-blossom viewing　☐ 健康診断 medical [physical] checkup　☐ みどりの日 Greenery Day　**5月**　☐ 憲法記念日 Constitution Day　☐ こどもの日 Children's Day　☐ こいのぼり carp streamers　**7月**　☐ 海の日 Marine Day　**8月**　☐ お盆 Bon Festival　☐ お中元 midsummer gifts　**9月**　☐ 敬老の日 Respect-for-the-Aged Day　☐ 秋分の日 Autumnal Equinox Day　☐ 月見 moon viewing　**10月**　☐ 体育の日 Health Sports Day　**11月**　☐ 文化の日 Culture Day　☐ 七五三 Seven-Five-Three Festival　☐ 勤労感謝の日 Labor Thanksgiving Day　**12月**　☐ 天皇誕生日 The Emperor's Birthday　☐ クリスマスイブ Christmas Eve　☐ サンタクロース Santa Claus　☐ トナカイ reindeers　☐ 御歳暮 year-end gifts　☐ 大みそか New Year's Eve　☐ 除夜の鐘 the tolling of the bells on New Year's Day　**1月**　☐ 元日 New Year's Day　☐ 年賀状 New Year's greeting cards　☐ 成人の日 Coming-of-Age Day　**2月**　☐ 節分 the traditional end of winter　☐ 建国記念日 National Foundation Day　**3月**　☐ ひな人形を飾る display dolls for Doll's Festival　☐ 春分の日 Vernal Equinox Day

〈日本文化 Japanese Culture〉

☐ 稲刈り cut rice　☐ 帯 sash　☐ お年玉 New Year's gift　☐ 華道 flower arrangement　☐ 着物 kimono　☐ 金魚すくいをする scoop goldfish　☐ 下駄 Japanese wooden sandals　☐ こけし kokeshi dolls　☐ 琴 koto harps　☐ 茶道 tea ceremony　☐ 三味線 shamisen　☐ 書道 calligraphy　☐ 太鼓をたたく beat a drum　☐ 田植えをする plant rice　☐ 足袋 Japanese-style socks　☐ 短歌 tanka　☐ 能 noh　☐ 俳句 haiku　☐ 初日の出 sunshine on the New Year's Day　☐ 花火大会 fireworks festival　☐ 羽根つき shuttlecock game　☐ 風呂敷 wrapping cloth　☐ 盆踊り Bon Festival dance　☐ 盆栽 bonsai [dwarf trees]　☐ 屋台 sidewalk stall　☐ 浴衣 light summer kimono　☐ 落語 comic storytelling　☐ 綿菓子 cotton candy

★ Words & Phrases ★

- Come and see me at my place over the weekend.（週末にうちに遊びにおいでよ）
- I had a very good time at the party.（パーティーはとても楽しかったよ）
- I bought cotton candy at a street stall.（僕は出店で綿菓子を買ったんだよ）
- My family visited my grandpa's grave.（私の家族はこの週末に祖父のお墓参りに行ってきました）
- Let's go buy Christmas present!（クリスマスプレゼントを買いに行こうよ）
- I have to buy some "friendship valentine" gifts.（あ～あ，義理チョコを買わなくちゃいけないの）

Topic 9 — 学校で / At School

School Buildings and Rooms

- ❶ school building 校舎
- ❷ school gate 校門
- ❸ playground 校庭
- ❹ parking lot 駐車場
- ❺ flower bed 花だん
- ❻ sand box 砂場
- ❼ entrance hall 玄関
- ❽ gym [gymnasium] 体育館
- ❾ swimming pool プール
- ❿ animal cage 飼育小屋
- ⓫ flagpole 国旗掲揚塔

- ① classroom 教室
- ② principal's room 校長室
- ③ teachers' room 職員室
- ④ nurse's office 保健室
- ⑤ office 事務室
- ⑥ science room [laboratory] 理科室
- ⑦ music room 音楽室
- ⑧ fine arts room [craft room] 美術室
- ⑨ computer room コンピュータ室
- ⑩ woodworking room 木工室
- ⑪ metalworking room 金工室
- ⑫ clothes-making room 被服室
- ⑬ cooking room 調理室
- ⑭ AV room 視聴覚室
- ⑮ all-purpose hall 多目的ホール
- ⑯ broadcasting room 放送室
- ⑰ restroom [bathroom] トイレ
- ⑱ counseling room 相談室

In the Classroom

- ① clock 時計
- ② (loud) speaker スピーカー
- ③ chalkboard [blackboard] 黒板
- ④ chalk チョーク
- ⑤ (chalkboard) eraser 黒板消し
- ⑥ computer コンピュータ
- ⑦ bulletin board [notice board] 掲示板
- ⑧ class schedule 時間割
- ⑨ window 窓
- ⑩ teacher's desk 教卓
- ⑪ bookshelf 本棚
- ⑫ desk 机
- ⑬ chair いす
- ⑭ overhead projector オーバーヘッドプロジェクター
- ⑮ fish tank 水槽
- ⑯ cleaning supplies closet 清掃用具入れ
- ⑰ wastebasket [trash can] ごみ箱
- ⑱ broom ほうき
- ⑲ dustpan ちりとり
- ⑳ floor cloth ぞうきん

- ❶ textbook 教科書
- ❷ notebook ノート
- ❸ pencil case 筆箱
- ❹ pencil 鉛筆
- ❺ red pen 赤ペン
- ❻ eraser 消しゴム
- ❼ pencil sharpener 鉛筆削り
- ❽ ruler 定規
- ❾ scissors はさみ
- ❿ glue のり
- ⓫ whiteout 修正液
- ⓬ loose-leaf paper ルーズリーフ用紙
- ⓭ binder バインダー
- ⓮ thumbtack 画びょう

Topic 10

授業やテストについて話そう！
What Is Your Favorite Subject?

● **Model Dialogue** ●

A: What subject do you like?
B: I like math. Do you like math, too?
A: No, not a bit.
B: Why not?
A: I don't understand functions. They're really difficult for me.
B: What is your favorite subject, then?
A: P.E. I like sports a lot.

A: どの教科が好き？
B: 数学。君も数学は好き？
A: 全然。
B: どうして？
A: 関数が分からないんだもん。すごい難しくて。
B: それじゃあどの教科が好きなの？
A: 体育だよ。スポーツ大好きだもん。

Class Schedule

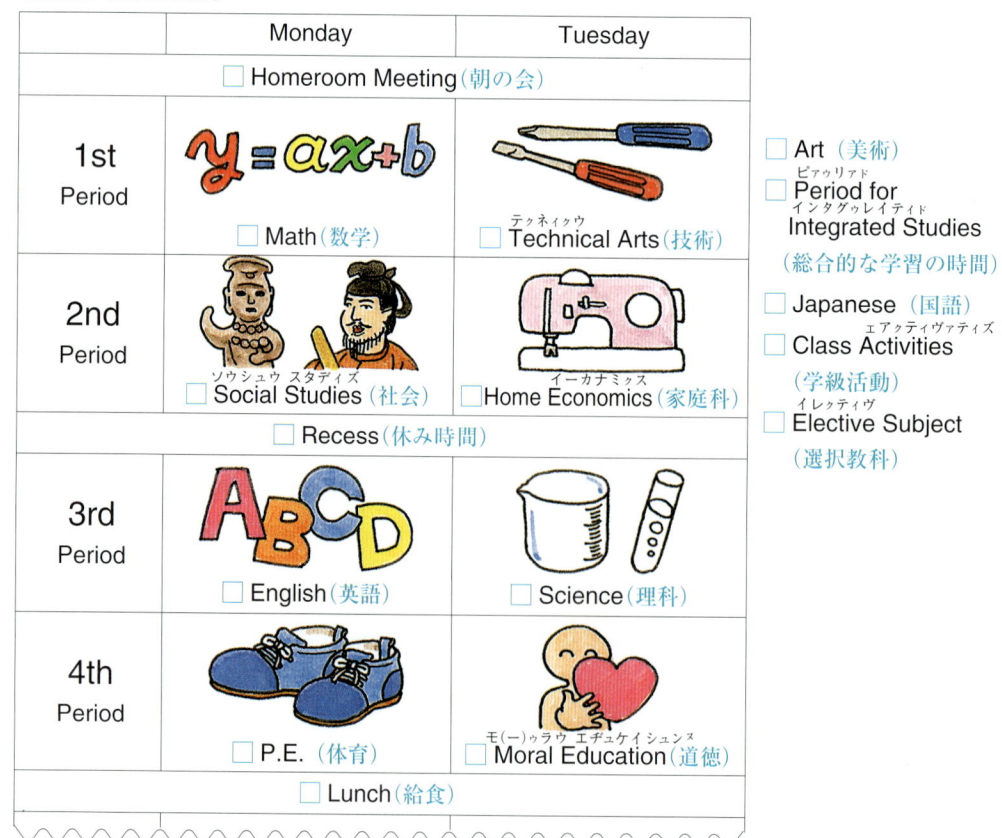

	Monday	Tuesday
	☐ Homeroom Meeting（朝の会）	
1st Period	☐ Math（数学）	☐ Technical Arts（技術）
2nd Period	☐ Social Studies（社会）	☐ Home Economics（家庭科）
	☐ Recess（休み時間）	
3rd Period	☐ English（英語）	☐ Science（理科）
4th Period	☐ P.E.（体育）	☐ Moral Education（道徳）
	☐ Lunch（給食）	

☐ Art（美術）
☐ Period for Integrated Studies（総合的な学習の時間）
☐ Japanese（国語）
☐ Class Activities（学級活動）
☐ Elective Subject（選択教科）

Part 2

○話題を広げよう！

＜例1＞自分の好きな教科，嫌いな教科→先生　➡ Topic 12，付録1 参照。

★ Words & Phrases ★

- ☐ 時間割 class schedule
- ☐ 期末テスト term-end [final] examination (イッゼアミネイシュンヌ)
- ☐ 教科書 textbook
- ☐ グループ学習 group work
- ☐ 黒板 chalkboard [blackboard]
- ☐ コンパス compass
- ☐ 作文 essay (エセイ)
- ☐ 自習時間 a free study period
- ☐ 辞書 dictionary
- ☐ 宿題 homework
- ☐ 定規 ruler (ゥルーラァ)
- ☐ 成績 grade [score] (グゥレイド スコー)
- ☐ 中間テスト midterm examination (ミドターム)
- ☐ 通知表 report card
- ☐ テスト test
- ☐ 読書感想文 book report
- ☐ プリント handout
- ☐ 補習 supplementary lesson (サプリマンタッリィ)
- ☐ ワーク workbook
- ☐ 暗記する memorize (メマゥライズ)
- ☐ 居眠りをする doze off (ドウズ)
- ☐ おしゃべりをする chat
- ☐ 答え合わせをする check the answer
- ☐ 答える answer the question
- ☐ 質問をする ask a question
- ☐ 手を挙げる raise my hand (ゥレイズ)
- ☐ ノートを取る take a note
- ☐ 話し合う discuss
- ☐ 復習する review (ゥリヴュー)
- ☐ 問題を解く solve a problem (サゥヴ プゥラブラム)
- ☐ 予習する prepare lessons (プゥリペァ レッスンズ)

★ Expressions in Use ★

- Your turn.（君の番だよ）
- Pass it to me, please.（私のところまで回してください）
- A: How was the test?（テストはどうだった？）
  B: Terrible.（最悪）(テゥラブゥ)
- Did you hand in the report?（レポートはもう提出した？）
- I got an "A" in math.（数学でAをとったよ）

★授業中に先生が使う主な指示

- 「答えを言って」Give the answer.
- 「答えを書いて」Write your answer.
- 「CDを聞いて」Listen to the CD.
- 「宿題を提出して」Hand in your homework.
- 「座りなさい」Sit down.
- 「立ちなさい」Stand up.
- 「手を挙げて」Raise your hands.
- 「ノートをとって」Take notes.
- 「本をしまって」Put away your books.
- 「本を開きなさい」Open your books.
- 「本を読みなさい」Read your books.

Topic 11

部活動について話そう！
What Club Are You In?

● **Model Dialogue** ●

A: What club are you in?
B: I'm on the baseball team. How about you?
A: I'm in the English club.
B: What do you do in your club?
A: Well, we usually read English books or watch some movies. How many students are there on your team?
B: About 30. We practice hard every day. We'd like to win our next game.

A: 何部に入っているの？
B: 野球部だよ。君は？
A: 英語部よ。
B: 部活でどんなことするの？
A: うーん，普段は英語の本を読んだり映画を見たり。ところであなたの部活は部員何人いるの？
B: 30人ぐらい。毎日きつい練習するんだ。今度の大会で優勝したいからね。

☐ **Sports Teams**（運動部）

☐ baseball team
（野球部）

☐ soccer [football] team（サッカー部）

☐ tennis team
（テニス部）

☐ volleyball team
（バレーボール部）

☐ basketball team
（バスケットボール部）

☐ table tennis [ping pong] team
（卓球部）

☐ softball team
（ソフトボール部）

☐ **Culture Clubs**（文化部）

☐ brass band
（吹奏楽部）

☐ chorus（コーラス）
（合唱部）

☐ computer club
（コンピュータ部）

Part 2

○話題を広げよう！

＜例1＞部活動の話→自分自身についての話→スポーツ選手や芸能人の話
　　　　　　　　　　　　　　　　　　　　　　　　➡ Topic 3, 6 参照。
＜例2＞部活動の話→友だちや先輩，顧問や担任の話　➡ Topic 12, 付録 4 参照。

★ Words & Phrases ★

- ☐ 演劇部 drama club
- ☐ 科学部 science club
- ☐ 華道部 flower arranging club
- ☐ 弓道部 Japanese archery team
- ☐ 茶道部 tea ceremony club
- ☐ 手芸部 handicrafts club
- ☐ 書道部 calligraphy club
- ☐ 新聞部 newspaper club
- ☐ 水泳部 swimming team
- ☐ 体操部 gymnastics team
- ☐ 美術部 art club
- ☐ 放送部 broadcasting club
- ☐ 陸上部 track and field team

- ☐ 朝練 morning practice
- ☐ 腕立て伏せ push up
- ☐ 合宿 training camp
- ☐ 監督 manager [coach]
- ☐ 気合い[精神] spirit
- ☐ 決勝 the finals
- ☐ 県大会 prefectural match
- ☐ 後輩 students younger than me
- ☐ 個人戦 individual match
- ☐ 顧問 adviser
- ☐ コンクール contest [competition]
- ☐ 根性 guts
- ☐ 試合 game [match]
- ☐ ジャージ jersey
- ☐ 柔軟体操 calisthenics
- ☐ 準決勝 the semi-finals
- ☐ 準備運動 warm-up
- ☐ 準優勝 runner-up
- ☐ 全国大会 all-Japan junior high school meet
- ☐ 先輩 students older than me
- ☐ 総当たり戦 round robin
- ☐ 体操着 athletic uniform
- ☐ 団体戦 team competition
- ☐ チームメート teammate
- ☐ チームワーク teamwork
- ☐ 展覧会 exhibition
- ☐ トーナメント tournament
- ☐ 特訓 special training
- ☐ トレーニング training
- ☐ 縄とび skipping rope
- ☐ 発表会 presentation
- ☐ 控え選手 reserve player
- ☐ 引き分け draw [tie]
- ☐ 部員 club member
- ☐ 部長 captain
- ☐ 腹筋運動 sit up
- ☐ マネージャー manager
- ☐ 優勝 victory
- ☐ ユニフォーム uniform
- ☐ 予選 heat
- ☐ リーグ戦 league match
- ☐ レギュラー選手 regular player
- ☐ 練習試合 practice match
- ☐ アドバイスを受ける get advice
- ☐ 引退する retire from a club
- ☐ 応援する cheer
- ☐ 着替える change into my school uniform [sportswear]
- ☐ けがをする get hurt
- ☐ 試合に出場する take part in a game
- ☐ 素振りをする practice my swings
- ☐ 退部する leave a club
- ☐ 入部する join a club
- ☐ 発表する present
- ☐ 引き分ける end in a draw
- ☐ ミーティングに出る attend a meeting
- ☐ 練習する practice

★ Expressions in Use ★

- I belong to the basketball team. [I'm a member of the basketball team. / I'm on the basketball team.]（私はバスケットボール部に入っています）
- We will play [have] a match [game] with Fujimi Junior High School tomorrow.
  （明日，富士見中学校と試合をします）
- I think (that) we're going to win [lose] the game [match].（私たちは試合に勝つ［負ける］と思う）
- Let's do our best!（全力を尽くそう！）

Topic 12

友だちや先生について話そう！
Your Friends and Teachers

● Model Dialogue ●

A: Who is your favorite teacher?
B: Um ... I like Ms. Suzuki.
A: Why?
B: Because she is gentle (デュエントウ) and kind. Which teacher do you like?
A: Oh, I like Mr. Tanaka the best.
B: Are you kidding? He is too strict (スチュイクト). I'm afraid (アフゥレイド) of him.
A: Oh, you don't know him well. He was my homeroom teacher last year. He took good care of us. And he is funny (ファネィ).
B: Is he? What do you think of Mr. Ito?
A: I think he is cool. A lot of the girls have a crush (クゥラシュ) on him.
B: But he has a girlfriend.
A: Really? I didn't know that.

A: 好きな先生だれ？
B: ええと，鈴木先生かなぁ。
A: なんで？
B: だって優しいし，親切だもん。あなたはどの先生が好き？
A: うーん田中先生が一番好き。
B: まさか。厳しすぎるわ。恐い。
A: あら，それはよく知らないからよ。去年担任だったんだ。生徒の面倒をよく見てくれたの。それに面白いし。
B: へえ，そうなんだ。伊藤先生どう思う？
A: かっこいいと思う。女の子にはかなり人気があるよね。
B: でも，先生，彼女いるんだよ。
A: ほんとに？ 知らなかったわ。

☐ homeroom teacher （学級担任）
☐ a member of the 〜 committee (カミティ) （〜委員）
☐ person in charge of 〜 (チュアーヂュ) （〜係）
☐ class president (プゥレズィダント) （学級委員）
☐ group leader （班長）
☐ student helpers today （日直）

Part 2

○話題を広げよう！
＜例1＞友だちの話→部活動の話→特技の話
＜例2＞先生の話→授業・テストの話→先生の性格の話

★ Words & Phrases ★

〈学校の先生や職員の人たち School Teachers and Staff〉

- □ 1年[2年／3年]の先生 teacher of first [second / third] grade
- □ ALTの先生 ALT
- □ 栄養士の先生 school nutritionist（ニューチュイシュネイスト）
- □ 学年の先生 teacher of our grade
- □ 給食調理員さん school cook
- □ 教頭先生 vice principal（ヴァイス プゥリンサプゥ）
- □ 校長先生 principal
- □ 事務の先生 school secretary（セクゥラテゥリィ）
- □ 相談員さん school counselor（カウンサラァ）
- □ 〜部の顧問の先生 adviser of 〜 club
- □ 養護の先生 school nurse
- □ 主事さん janitor（デュェアネイタァ）

〈外見や性格 Appearance and Personalities〉

- □ 明るく元気な cheerful [happy / bright]
- □ 頭がいい smart
- □ 頭がはげている bald（ボーゥド）
- □ いじめっ子 bully（ブリィ）
- □ えこひいきをする unfair（アンフェア）
- □ 怒りっぽい touchy（タチュイ）
- □ おしゃれな stylish
- □ おデブちゃん chubby（チュアビィ）
- □ 思いやりがある considerate（カンスィダレト）
- □ かっこいい cool
- □ がっちりした chunky（チュアンキィ）
- □ 我慢強い patient（ペイシュント）
- □ かわいい cute
- □ 厳しい strict
- □ 暗い gloomy（グルーミィ）
- □ 公平な fair
- □ 社交的な friendly
- □ 楽しい fun
- □ だらしない messy（メスィ）
- □ 天才 genius（デューイーニァス）
- □ 年をとっている old
- □ 恥ずかしがりや shy（シュアイ）
- □ 控えめな modest（マディスト）
- □ ほっそりした slender
- □ 前向きな positive（パズィティヴ）
- □ 真面目な serious（スィアゥリアス）
- □ もの静かな quiet
- □ 優しい kind [gentle]
- □ 若い young

★ Expressions in Use ★

- He is very popular with girls.（彼はとても女の子にもてる）
- She has quick temper.（彼女は短気だ）
- Mr. Toyoda always looks after the students with tender.
  （豊田先生は生徒のことに親身になって考えてくれるんだ）

★覚えておこう！「先生！」

日本語では先生を呼ぶとき，「宮本先生」のように名前のあとに「先生」を付けますが，英語では Miyamoto teacher という言い方はしません。Mr. Miyamoto や Ms. Yoshida のように，名前で呼びます。また，何か用があって声をかけるときも，日本語では「先生」と呼びかけるのに対して，英語では名前で呼びかけます。

Topic 13: 修学旅行や林間学校について話そう！
Let's Talk about School Trips!

● **Model Dialogue** ●

A: What is your best memory of the school trip?
B: Well, the pillow(ピロウ) fight was the best. But we got caught(コート). Mr. Tanaka scolded(スコウディド) us.
A: Really?
B: How about your best memory?
A: The Great Image of Buddha in Nara was my best. It was so huge(ヒューヂュ)! I was impressed(イムプゥレスト).

A: 修学旅行の一番の思い出は何ですか。
B: そうね……まくら投げが一番だったよ。でも，先生に見つかっちゃった。田中先生におこられちゃった。
A: 本当に？
B: あなたの一番の思い出は？
A: 奈良の大仏だな。あまりに巨大で，これには驚いたよ。

- temple（寺）
- image of Buddha(ブダァ)（仏像）
- admission fee(アドミシュンス)（拝観料）
- entrance(エンチュァンス)（入口）
- souvenir(スーヴァネィァ)（おみやげ）
- No Photography（撮影禁止）

○話題を広げよう！

＜例1＞修学旅行の話→自由行動の話→食事の話　　➡ Topic 7 参照。
＜例2＞思い出の話→友だちの話→先生の話　　　　➡ Topic 12 参照。

★ Words & Phrases ★

- ☐ 修学旅行 school trip
- ☐ 観光地 sightseeing spot
- ☐ ガイド guide
- ☐ 地図 map
- ☐ おみやげ屋さん souvenir shop
- ☐ 特産物 special products
- ☐ 手荷物 baggage
- ☐ 旅行のしおり guide for trip
- ☐ 添乗員 tour conductor
- ☐ バスの運転手 bus driver
- ☐ 修学旅行専用列車 special train for school trips
- ☐ 観光バス sightseeing bus
- ☐ 新幹線 super express
- ☐ 旅館 Japanese-style hotel
- ☐ 浴衣 light summer kimono
- ☐ かけぶとん quilt
- ☐ しきぶとん mattress
- ☐ 城 castle
- ☐ 天守閣 donjon
- ☐ 石垣 stone wall
- ☐ 屋根瓦 roofing
- ☐ 神社 shrine
- ☐ 五重塔 five-storied pagoda
- ☐ 僧侶 priest
- ☐ 袈裟 Buddhist priest's kimono
- ☐ 大仏 the great image of Buddha
- ☐ 参道 entrance path
- ☐ 舞妓 apprentice *geisha*
- ☐ 遠足 field day
- ☐ 臨海学校 school camp by the sea
- ☐ スキー旅行 ski trip
- ☐ 林間学校 school camp in the mountain
- ☐ おやつ refreshments
- ☐ 軽食 snack
- ☐ キャンプ場 camping ground
- ☐ キャンプ用品 camping outfit
- ☐ 水筒 water bottle
- ☐ 懐中電灯 flashlight
- ☐ リュックサック backpack
- ☐ 寝袋 sleeping bag
- ☐ ハンドマイク hand-mike
- ☐ スナップ写真を撮る take a snap shot
- ☐ 点呼をとる take a head count
- ☐ ～の係り student responsible for ～
- ☐ 班行動をする go around in groups
- ☐ 自由行動をする be free
- ☐ ～へ遠足に行く make a trip to ～
- ☐ キャンプに行く go camping
- ☐ 登山する go mountain climbing
- ☐ キャンプファイヤーをする make a campfire

★ Expressions in Use ★

- What was your first impression of Kyoto?（京都の第一印象はどうでしたか）
- Ken and I developed a stronger bond with friends.（健と私は友情をはぐくんだ）
- *A:* What place did you like the best?（気に入った場所はどこでしたか）
  B: I liked Kinkakuji the best.（金閣寺です）
- *A:* What did you eat for lunch?（お昼に何を食べましたか）
  B: We ate *yudofu*.（私たちは湯豆腐を食べました）
- *A:* What souvenirs did you buy?（お土産は何を買いましたか）
  B: I bought *yatsuhashi* and a Japanese fan.（八橋と扇子を買いました）
- *A:* Did you sleep well at the hotel?（ホテルではよく眠れましたか）
  B: I couldn't stand his snoring [gnash].（彼のいびき［歯ぎしり］はがまんできなかった）

Topic 14

体育祭や合唱祭について話そう！
Field Day and Chorus Contest

● **Model Dialogue** ●

A: What part of field day do you like the best?
B: I like the inter-class relays the best.
A: Why do you like it the best?
B: It's exciting. How about you? What do you like the best?
A: I like the obstacle race. It's fun!
B: I agree.

A: 体育祭で何が一番好き？
B: クラス対抗リレーだよ。
A: どうして一番好きなの？
B: 興奮するよね。君はどうなの？何が一番好き？
A: 障害物競走が一番いいよ。面白いもん。
B: 同感！

- ① field day（体育祭）
- ② playground（校庭）
- ③ relay（リレー）
- ④ main tent（本部席）
- ⑤ score board（得点板）
- ⑥ broadcasting corner（放送席）
- ⑦ cheer（応援する）

○話題を広げよう！

＜例１＞体育祭の話→競技・クラスの話→先生・友だち・先輩の話
＜例２＞合唱曲の話→音楽の話→趣味・特技の話

★ Words & Phrases ★

〈体育祭 Field Day〉

- ☐ 石につまずいて転ぶ stumble over a stone
- ☐ 運動靴 sneakers
- ☐ (〜に)気合を入れろ Put more guts into 〜
- ☐ 競争に参加する compete in a race
- ☐ 記録係 person in charge of recording the score
- ☐ 種目 program
- ☐ 障害物競走 obstacle race
- ☐ ゼッケン (player's) number
- ☐ 退場門 exit (gate)
- ☐ 体操服 athletic uniform
- ☐ 玉ころがし big ball rolling race
- ☐ テント tent
- ☐ 得点 score
- ☐ 跳び箱 vaulting horse
- ☐ 二人三脚 three-legged race
- ☐ 入場門 entrance (gate)
- ☐ はしご ladder
- ☐ 万国旗 flags of all nations
- ☐ 100メートル走 100-meter dash [race]
- ☐ フォークダンス folk dance
- ☐ 袋競争 sack race
- ☐ 誘導係 person in charge of leading the players
- ☐ ライン引き line drawing machine
- ☐ ラジオ体操 radio gymnastics

〈合唱祭 Chorus Contest〉

- ☐ １位になる win first prize
- ☐ 音痴 sing off key
- ☐ 音程が狂っている sing out of tune
- ☐ 音程がしっかりしている sing in tune
- ☐ 開会式 opening ceremony
- ☐ 課題曲 required chorus
- ☐ 観客 audience
- ☐ 校歌 school song
- ☐ 司会 master of ceremonies
- ☐ 指揮者 conductor
- ☐ 実行委員会 working committee
- ☐ 自由曲 optional song
- ☐ 審査委員 judge
- ☐ 団結 union
- ☐ 伴奏 accompaniment
- ☐ 伴奏者 accompanist
- ☐ 舞台 stage
- ☐ 閉会式 closing ceremony
- ☐ マイク microphone
- ☐ やじ booing
- ☐ 練習 practice

★ Expressions in Use ★

- A: How was the field day?（体育祭はどうでしたか）
  B: It was great. Our class won the field day.
  （素晴らしかったです。私たち，体育祭で優勝しました）
- I think we won because of Ken.（ケンのおかげで勝ったと思います）
- A: What do you think of the field day?（体育祭についてどう思いますか）
  B: I can't stand it! I hate field day because I'm a slow runner.
  （最低です。私は運動会がきらいです。なぜなら，私は走るのが遅いからです）
- Good try, Takao.（気にしないで，タカオ）
- Yeah! Yeah!（やった，やった！）
- We lost.（負けてしまいました）
- I'm not good at music.（私は音楽が苦手だ）
- The class joined up to sing a song (together).（クラスが団結して合唱した）
- The whole class joined together as one.（クラスが１つになった）
- I was touched by the chorus contest.（合唱祭は私を感動させた）
- A split in my class lost the chorus contest for us.（クラスが分裂したので合唱祭に負けた）
- The boys in my class are always having fun.（うちのクラスの男子たちはふざけてばかりいる）

Topic 15

買い物に行こう！
Let's Go Shopping!

● **Model Dialogue** ●

Clerk: Hello. May I help you?
Guest: Yes. Show me that blue jacket, please. Do you have it in my size?
Clerk: Sure. How about this?
Guest: Can I try it on?
Clerk: Go ahead. How do you like it?
Guest: It fits me perfectly.
Clerk: It suits you.
Guest: Thank you. How much is it?
Clerk: 140 dollars.
Guest: 140 dollars? That's too expensive.
Clerk: How about this black one? It's only 105 dollars.
Guest: OK. I'll take it.

C: こんにちは。いらっしゃいませ。
G: はい。あの青いジャケットを見せてください。私に合うサイズありますか。
C: ええ。これはいかがですか。
G: 試着してみてもいいですか。
C: どうぞ。いかがですか。
G: 私にちょうどいいみたいです。
C: お似合いですよ。
G: ありがとう。これ、いくらですか？
C: 140ドルです。
G: 140ドル？ ちょっと高すぎるなぁ。
C: この黒いほうはいかがですか。こちらなら105ドルです。
G: いいですね。それ、いただきます。

○話題を広げよう！

＜例1＞趣味の話→買い物の話→ファッションの話　➡　Topic 3, 6 参照。
＜例2＞買い物の話→まち(お店)の話→料理の話　➡　Topic 2, 7 参照。

★ Words & Phrases ★

- □ きつい tight (タイト)
- □ 手ごろな値段の reasonable (ゥリーズナブゥ)
- □ 売り切れ sold out
- □ 価格 price
- □ 食料品店 grocery shop (グゥロウサゥリィ)
- □ デパート department store (ディパートマント)
- □ フリーサイズ one size fits all

- □ ゆるい loose (ルーズ)
- □ 安い cheap (チゥイープ)
- □ 営業時間 store hours
- □ 化粧品 cosmetics (カズメティクズ)
- □ スーパー supermarket
- □ 店員 clerk
- □ 洋服 clothing

- □ 高い expensive (イクスペンスィヴ)
- □ 衣料品店 clothing shop (クロウズィング)
- □ おみやげ店 souvenir shop (スーヴァネィア)
- □ 試着室 fitting room (フィティング)
- □ セール中 on sale
- □ 日用品 daily necessities (ナセサティズ)
- □ レジ cash register (ゥレヂュイスタァ)

★ Expressions in Use ★

- What colors do you have?（何色がありますか？）
- These pants are too tight.（このズボンきつすぎます）
- What do you recommend?（何がおすすめですか？）(ゥレカメンド)
- Anything else?（ほかに何かお求めは）
- Can I exchange this?（取り換えてもらえますか？）(イクスチュエインヂュ)
- Nothing for me, thanks.（欲しいものがありません）
- What is this made of?（何で出来ているのですか？）
- A: May I help you? What are you looking for?（いらっしゃいませ。何をお探しですか？）
  B: I'm just looking.（見てるだけです）
  A: If you need any help, let me know.（ご用がありましたらお知らせください）
- A: Where is the food hall?（食品売り場はどこですか）
  B: It's on the second floor.（2階です）
- A: Please show me another style. It's too loud.
  （他のデザインを見せてください。派手すぎです）
  B: How do you like this?（これなんかいかがですか）
  A: I'll think about it.（もう少し考えます）
- A: Do you have any smaller [larger] size? This is too large [small].
  （もう少し小さい[大きい]サイズありますか。これは大きすぎ[小さすぎ]ます）
  B: How about this one?（これはどうですか）
  A: It's the right size.（ピッタリです）
- A: Which is better?（どっちがいいと思う）
  B: This is better. You should get it.（これがいいよ。絶対買ったほうがいいよ）
  A: I want both of them.（両方欲しいな）

Topic 16

電話でデートに誘おう!
Talking on the Phone

● **Model Dialogue** ●

Lisa: Hello?
Ken: Hello. This is Ken. Can I speak to Lisa, please?
Lisa: Speaking.
Ken: Oh, hi, Lisa. How are you doing?
Lisa: Great. Well, what's up?
Ken: I have two tickets (ティキッ) for a Japan-Brazil game next Saturday. Shall we go together? (タゲザァ)
Lisa: Wow. Sounds great. I'd love to.
Ken: I'll see you at the station at five then.
Lisa: Thank you for calling (コーリング). Bye.

L: もしもし。
K: もしもし。健ですけど, リサはいますか？
L: 私ですけど。
K: やあ, リサ。元気？
L: 元気よ。どうしたの？
K: 土曜日の日本対ブラジル戦のチケットが手に入ったんだ。いっしょに見にいかない？
L: すごいじゃない。いいわねぇ。ぜひ。
K: 5時に駅で待ち合わせようよ。
L: 電話, ありがとう。じゃあね。

● **話したい相手がいなくて伝言を残す場合**

① Hello? This is Ken speaking. May I speak to Lisa, please?

② Lisa is out right now. She'll be back around six.

③ Can I leave a message?
Sure.

④ Please ask her to call me back. My number is ～.

★ Words & Phrases ★

- 緊急電話 emergency call
- 携帯電話 cellphone [cellular phone / mobile phone]
- 公衆電話 public telephone
- 国際電話 international call
- 市外局番 area code
- 市内通話 local call
- 受話器を取る pick up the phone
- 長距離電話 long distance call
- 伝言 message
- 電話 telephone [phone]
- 電話帳 phone book
- 電話を切る hang up
- 発信音 dial tone
- 話し中 The line is busy.
- 間違い電話 wrong number
- メモを取る take notes
- 留守番電話 answering machine

★ Expressions in Use ★

〈電話〉

- I'm sorry I have the wrong number. （すいません。番号を間違えました）
- I have another call. （キャッチホンが入りました）
- Sorry to call you so late. （こんなに遅くにごめんなさい）
- Hold on, please. （お待ちください）
- Who's calling please? （どちらさまですか？）
- Please tell Nancy I called. （ナンシーに電話があったことお伝えください）
- Can I take a message? （伝言はございますか？）
- I'll have him call you as soon as he comes back. （帰りしだい，電話させます）
- May I have your number? （あなたの電話番号を教えてください）
- A: Ken isn't at home. （健は家におりません）
  B: When will he be back? （何時に戻りますか？）
  A: He'll be back around six. （6時ごろ戻ります）
  B: I'll call back again. （また電話します）
- A: I have to go now. （そろそろ失礼します）
  B: Nice talking to you. Bye! （話が出来てよかったです。じゃあね）

〈誘い〉

- Do you have any plans? （何か予定ある？）
- Could you give me the date and time? （日時を教えてください）
- Where [When / What time] shall we meet? （どこで［いつ／何時に］会おうか？）
- I'm free from three to four thirty. （3時から4時半までなら空いているよ）
- Shall we ～? / How about ～ ing? / Why don't we ～? （～しませんか？）
- A: What are you doing now? （今，何してるの？）
  B: Nothing. （別に）
- A: Are you free this Sunday afternoon? （今週の日曜日の午後は空いている？）
  B: Sorry. I already have plans. （ダメなんです。もう予定が入っています）

Topic 17 道案内をしよう！
Asking the Way

● **Model Dialogues** ●

A

A: Excuse me. Where is the post office?
B: Let me see. Walk along this street and turn right at the first traffic light. (チュエアフィク)
A: The first light?
B: Yes. A big building (ビウディング) is on your left. The post office is next to it.
A: Thank you very much.
B: Not at all.

A: すみません。郵便局はどこですか？
B: ええと。この通りをまっすぐ行って，最初の信号を右に曲がってください。
A: 最初の信号ですね？
B: はい。すると大きな建物が左手に見えますから，その隣が郵便局です。
A: ありがとうございました。
B: どういたしまして。

B

A: Excuse me. Could you tell me the way to City Hall?
B: Well, it's far from here. You should (シュド) go by train.
A: Which train should I take?
B: Take the Chuo Line for Yuhigaoka.
A: And where should I get off?
B: At Higashi Station. City Hall is near the station.
A: Oh, I see. Thank you very much.
B: You're welcome.

A: すみません。市役所へはどうやって行けばよいのですか？
B: ここからは遠いですよ。電車で行ったほうがいいですよ。
A: どの電車に乗るのですか？
B: 夕日が丘行きの中央線に乗ってください。
A: どこで降りるのですか？
B: 東駅ですよ。市役所は駅の近くですから。
A: 分かりました。どうもありがとうございました。
B: いいえ，どういたしまして。

★ Words & Phrases ★

- ☐ 横断歩道 pedestrian crossing
- ☐ 改札口 ticket gate
- ☐ 角 corner
- ☐ 観光案内所 tourist information
- ☐ 観光スポット tourist spot
- ☐ 切符売り場 ticket office
- ☐ コインロッカー coin-operated locker
- ☐ 時刻表 timetable
- ☐ 自動券売機 ticket machine
- ☐ 出発時刻 departure time
- ☐ 信号機 traffic light
- ☐ 地下鉄 subway
- ☐ 近道 shortcut
- ☐ 電車 train
- ☐ 到着時刻 arrival time
- ☐ 乗り換える transfer
- ☐ バス bus
- ☐ バス停 bus stop
- ☐ ブロック block
- ☐ 歩道橋 pedestrian overpass
- ☐ 路線図 route map
- ☐ 路面電車 streetcar
- ☐ ～行き bound for ～
- ☐ ～の角 at the corner of ～
- ☐ ～の近くに near ～
- ☐ ～の前 in front of ～
- ☐ ～の向かい側 opposite to ～
- ☐ ～を越えて across ～
- ☐ ～を突き当たって at the end of ～
- ☐ あそこの～ ～ over there
- ☐ 最初の曲がり角 at the first corner
- ☐ まっすぐ行く go straight
- ☐ 右[左]側に on your right [left]
- ☐ 右[左]に曲がる turn right [left]

★ Expressions in Use ★

[道案内編]

- Are there any landmarks?（何か目印はありますか？）
- How far is the park from here?（その公園までどのくらいありますか？）
- A: Could you tell me the way to the post office?（郵便局への行き方を教えてください）

  B: Go straight and turn left over there. You'll see the post office on your right.

  （まっすぐ行って，あそこで左に曲がります。右側に郵便局が見えてきます）

- A: How long will it take?（どれくらい時間がかかりますか？）

  B: It's only about ten minutes' walk from here.（ここから歩いてほんの10分くらいの距離です）

- A: Is there a post office near here?（このあたりに郵便局はありますか？）

  B: Sorry, I don't know, either.（すみません，私もよく分からないのです）

[電車・バス編]

- How many stations [stops] is it from here?（いくつ目の駅[停留所]ですか？）
- Where should I get on [off]?（どこで乗れば[降りれば]いいのですか？）
- Change trains at Yokohama Station.（横浜駅で乗り換えなさい）
- A: Does this train stop at Yurakucho?（この電車は有楽町に止まりますか？）

  B: No. Get off at Tokyo Station and change to the Yamanote Line.

  （いいえ。東京駅で降りて山手線に乗り換えます）

- A: Which bus should I take to Chinatown?（中華街へはどのバスに乗ればいいのですか？）

  B: Take the number 2 or 3 bus.（2番か3番のバスに乗ってください）

Topic 18

困難を切り抜けよう！
Let's Overcome Our Difficulties!

● **Model Dialogues** ●

A

A: You look pale (ペイウ). What's the matter?
B: I feel sick. I think I have a fever (フィーヴァ).
A: Let me check. You'd better go home.
B: Maybe (メイビ(ー)). I have a chill (チュイウ) now.
A: Did you take any medicine (メディスンヌ)?
B: No. But I'll go see the school nurse.

A: 顔色悪いよ。どうしたの？
B: 気分がすぐれないくて，熱があるみたい。
A: ちょっと見せて。帰ったほうがいいよ。
B: そうかもしれない。寒気もするんだ。
A: 何か薬飲んだ？
B: いいえ。でも，保健室に行ってみる。

B

A: I left my bag here, but now it's gone (ゴ(ー)ンヌ).
B: When did you last see it?
A: Just ten minutes ago.
B: What's inside?
A: My passport and some money.
B: You better go to the police and the Embassy (エムバスィ).
A: That's right. I have to get a new passport.

A: かばんをここに置いたのですが，なくなってしまいました。
B: 最後に見たのはいつですか。
A: 10分ほど前です。
B: 中身は何ですか。
A: パスポートとお金です。
B: 警察と大使館に行ったほうがいいですよ。
A: そうです。私はパスポートを再発行してもらわなければなりません。

★ Words & Phrases ★

[病気・不調編]

- ☐ 応急手当 first aid (エイド)
- ☐ かすり傷 scratch (スクゥレアチュ)
- ☐ 風邪 cold
- ☐ 花粉症 hay fever (ヘイ フィーヴァ)
- ☐ かゆみ itch (イチュ)
- ☐ 筋肉痛 muscle ache (マスゥ エイク)
- ☐ くしゃみ sneeze (スニーズ)
- ☐ 骨折 fracture (フゥレアクチュア)
- ☐ 時差ぼけ jet lag
- ☐ 症状 symptom (スィムプタム)
- ☐ 食中毒 food poisoning (ポイズニング)
- ☐ 筋を違える strain (スチュエインス)
- ☐ 食欲がない have no appetite (エアピタイト)
- ☐ 診察 see a doctor
- ☐ 打撲 blow (ブロウ)
- ☐ 突き指 sprained finger
- ☐ 日射病 sunstroke
- ☐ ねんざ sprain
- ☐ 鼻水 runny nose (ゥラニィ)
- ☐ ばんそうこう Band-Aid (ベアンデイド)
- ☐ 包帯 bandage (ベアンディヂュ)
- ☐ 虫さされ insect bite (インセクト バイト)
- ☐ やけど burn

★ Expressions in Use ★

- A: Do you feel sick? You don't look well. (どこか具合悪いの？ いつもと違うよ)

  B: I have a stomachache. (スタマケイク) (おなかが痛いんです)

  I can't stop coughing. (コフィング) (せきが止まりません)

  I have hay fever. (花粉症にかかった)

  I have diarrhea. (ダイァゥリァ) (下痢なんだ)

  I feel nauseous. (ノーズィァス) (はきけがします)

  I was bitten by a mosquito. It itches. (ビトンス) (マスキートゥ) (蚊に刺されました。かゆいです)

- A: I hope you feel better soon. (早くよくなるといいですね)

[盗難・紛失編]

- A: What happened? (どうなさいました)

  B: I lost my key. (かぎをなくしました)

  My wallet was stolen. (ワリト) (ストウランス) (財布を盗まれました)

  I left my bag on the bus. (バスの中にカバンを置き忘れました)

  I can't find my baggage. (ベアギヂュ) (荷物が出てきません)

★緊急のときのかけ声

- Look [Watch] out! (危ない！)
- Freeze! (フゥリーズ) (動くな！)
- Fire! (火事だぁ！)
- Hands off! (手を離せ！)
- Get down! (伏せろ！)
- Emergency! (イマーヂュァンスィ) (緊急です)
- Hold it! (止まれ！)

付録 1　人に関する表現

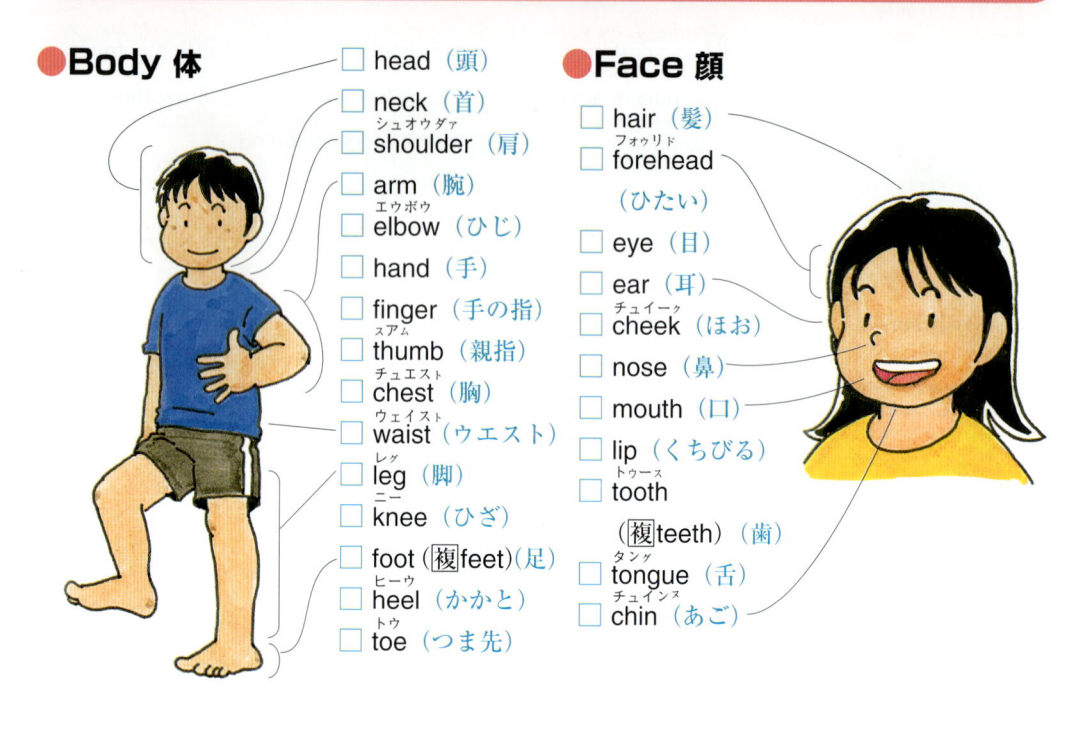

●Body 体
- ☐ head（頭）
- ☐ neck（首）
- ☐ shoulder（肩）シュオウダァ
- ☐ arm（腕）エゥボゥ
- ☐ elbow（ひじ）
- ☐ hand（手）
- ☐ finger（手の指）
- ☐ thumb（親指）スアム
- ☐ chest（胸）チュエスト
- ☐ waist（ウエスト）ウェイスト
- ☐ leg（脚）レグ
- ☐ knee（ひざ）ニー
- ☐ foot（複feet）（足）
- ☐ heel（かかと）ヒーゥ
- ☐ toe（つま先）トゥ

●Face 顔
- ☐ hair（髪）
- ☐ forehead（ひたい）フォゥリド
- ☐ eye（目）
- ☐ ear（耳）
- ☐ cheek（ほお）チューク
- ☐ nose（鼻）
- ☐ mouth（口）
- ☐ lip（くちびる）
- ☐ tooth（複teeth）（歯）トゥース
- ☐ tongue（舌）タング
- ☐ chin（あご）チュインヌ

●外見を表す表現

- ☐ 美しい beautiful
- ☐ おデブちゃんな chubby チュアビィ
- ☐ がりがりの bony ボゥニィ
- ☐ きれいな pretty
- ☐ 上品な elegant エリガント
- ☐ 華やかな gorgeous ゴージャス
- ☐ ほっそりした slender スレンダァ
- ☐ やせっぽちの skinny スキニィ

- ☐ 大きい big
- ☐ かっこいい cool
- ☐ かわいい cute
- ☐ 子どもっぽい，幼稚な（けなして）childish チュアイゥディシュ
- ☐ ぞっとする creepy
- ☐ ふくよかな plump プラムプ
- ☐ 魅力的な attractive アチュエアクティヴ
- ☐ やせている thin スインヌ

- ☐ おしゃれな stylish スタイリシュ
- ☐ がっちりした chunky チュアンキィ
- ☐ きりっとした handsome
- ☐ のっぽでやせっぽちの lanky レアンキィ
- ☐ 太った fat
- ☐ 魅力的な，セクシーな sexy

●性格を表す表現

- ☐ 明るい cheerful チュアフゥ
- ☐ おしゃべりな talkative トーカティヴ
- ☐ 思いやりがある considerate カンスィダレト
- ☐ 勝ち気な tough タフ
- ☐ けちな stingy スティンヂュイ
- ☐ 上品で優しい gentle
- ☐ 辛抱強い patient ペイシュント
- ☐ 繊細な delicate デリキト
- ☐ 恥ずかしがりやな shy シュアイ
- ☐ 朗らかな happy
- ☐ 弱い weak

- ☐ 意地悪な mean ミーンヌ
- ☐ 落ち込んでいる depressed ディプゥレスト
- ☐ おもしろい funny ファニィ
- ☐ きびしい strict スチュイクト
- ☐ 強引な pushy プシュイ
- ☐ 神経質な nervous ナーヴァス
- ☐ 性格の悪い evil
- ☐ 短気な short-tempered シュオートテムパァド
- ☐ 控えめな modest マデストゥ
- ☐ 前向きな positive パズィティヴ
- ☐ わがままな spoiled スポイゥド

- ☐ いばっている arrogant エアゥラガント
- ☐ おとなしい，静かな quiet クゥワイァト
- ☐ かしこい smart スマート
- ☐ 気楽な easygoing
- ☐ 社交的な friendly
- ☐ 親切な kind
- ☐ せかせかした restless ゥレストラス
- ☐ 泣き虫な crybaby クゥライベイビィ
- ☐ 太っ腹な generous ヂュエナゥラス
- ☐ 優しい sweet

付録2　物を表す表現

● Shapes and Figures 形

- ☐ triangle チュアイェアングゥ（三角形）
- ☐ circle サークゥ（円）
- ☐ square スクウェア（正方形）
- ☐ 円すい cone コウンス
- ☐ 円柱 cylinder スィリンダァ
- ☐ 球 sphere スフィア
- ☐ 五角形 pentagon ペンタガン
- ☐ 四角すい pyramid ピュラミド
- ☐ 台形 trapezoid チュアペゾイド
- ☐ だ円 oval オウヴォゥ
- ☐ 長方形 rectangle ゥレクテアングゥ
- ☐ 直角三角形 right triangle ゥライト
- ☐ ひし形 diamond ダイアマンド
- ☐ 立方体 cube キューブ

● Colors 色

① ② ③ ④ ⑤ ⑥ ⑦ ⑧ ⑨ ⑩

- ☐ ①青 blue
- ☐ ②赤 red
- ☐ ③黄色 yellow
- ☐ ④黒 black
- ☐ ⑤白 white
- ☐ ⑥茶色 brown
- ☐ ⑦緑 green
- ☐ ⑧紫 purple パープゥ
- ☐ ⑨灰色 gray
- ☐ ⑩ピンク pink

- ☐ 金 gold
- ☐ 銀 silver
- ☐ 水色 light blue
- ☐ こげ茶色 dark brown
- ☐ 黄緑 yellow green

● 色・大きさ・長さ・量など

- ☐ long（長い）
- ☐ short（短い）
- ☐ big（大きい）
- ☐ small（小さい）
- ☐ heavy ヘヴィ（重い）
- ☐ light（軽い）

- ☐ hot（暑い）
- ☐ cold（寒い）
- ☐ fast（速い）
- ☐ slow（ゆっくりとした）
- ☐ thick スィク（厚い／太い）
- ☐ thin スィンス（薄い／細い）

反対語リスト

- ☐ new（新しい） ⇔ ☐ old（古い）
- ☐ good（良い） ⇔ ☐ bad（悪い）
- ☐ soft（柔らかい） ⇔ ☐ hard（かたい）
- ☐ noisy ノイズィ（うるさい） ⇔ ☐ quiet クワイアト（静かな）
- ☐ easy（易しい） ⇔ ☐ hard [difficult]（難しい）
- ☐ interesting（面白い） ⇔ ☐ boring ボーゥリング（つまらない）
- ☐ deep（深い） ⇔ ☐ shallow シェアロウ（浅い）
- ☐ dry デュライ（乾いた） ⇔ ☐ wet ウェト（ぬれた）
- ☐ young（若い） ⇔ ☐ old（年をとった）
- ☐ beautiful（美しい） ⇔ ☐ ugly アグリィ（みにくい）
- ☐ high（高い） ⇔ ☐ low（低い）
- ☐ cool（涼しい） ⇔ ☐ warm（暖かい）
- ☐ clean（きれいな） ⇔ ☐ dirty ダーティ（汚い）
- ☐ light（光が明るい） ⇔ ☐ dark（暗い）
- ☐ cheap チューブ（安い） ⇔ ☐ expensive イクスペンスィヴ（高価な）
- ☐ wide（幅が広い） ⇔ ☐ narrow ネアゥロウ（狭い）
- ☐ tall（背が高い） ⇔ ☐ short（背が低い）
- ☐ early（早い） ⇔ ☐ late（遅い）
- ☐ strong（強い） ⇔ ☐ weak（弱い）
- ☐ near（近い） ⇔ ☐ far（遠い）

付録 3　生き物や食べ物

●Animals 動物

- ☐ cat（ネコ）
- ☐ horse（馬）
- ☐ rabbit（ウサギ）
- ☐ dog（犬）
- ☐ pig（豚）
- ☐ bear（クマ）
- ☐ elephant（ゾウ）
- ☐ cow（牛）
- ☐ sheep（羊）
- ☐ mouse（ネズミ）
- ☐ lion（ライオン）
- ☐ tiger（トラ）
- ☐ オオカミ wolf （ウゥフ）
- ☐ オランウータン orangutan（オーゥレアンガーテアンス）
- ☐ カバ hippopotamus（ヒパパタマス）
- ☐ カメ turtle（タートゥ）
- ☐ カンガルー kangaroo
- ☐ キツネ fox
- ☐ キリン giraffe
- ☐ コアラ koala
- ☐ シカ deer
- ☐ シマウマ zebra
- ☐ スカンク skunk
- ☐ タヌキ raccoon dog（ゥレアクーンス）
- ☐ パンダ panda
- ☐ ヘビ snake
- ☐ モグラ mole（モウ）
- ☐ ヤギ goat
- ☐ ラクダ camel
- ☐ ロバ donkey
- ☐ ワニ alligator / crocodile（エァリゲイタァ クゥラカダイゥ）

●Birds 鳥

- ☐ chicken / hen（雌鳥）（めんどり）
- ☐ rooster（雄鳥）（ウルースタァ）（おんどり）
- ☐ swallow（ツバメ）
- ☐ sparrow（スズメ）（スペアゥロゥ）
- ☐ crow（カラス）
- ☐ owl（フクロウ）（アゥゥ）
- ☐ eagle（ワシ）
- ☐ peacock（クジャク）
- ☐ アヒル duck
- ☐ インコ parakeet（ペァゥラキート）
- ☐ オウム parrot
- ☐ ガチョウ goose（グース）／複 geese（ギース）
- ☐ かもめ sea gull（ガゥ）
- ☐ 七面鳥 turkey（ターキィ）
- ☐ タカ hawk
- ☐ ダチョウ ostrich（オ(ー)ストゥイチュ）
- ☐ 白鳥 swan
- ☐ ハト pigeon（ピヂュアンス）
- ☐ ペンギン penguin

●Fish and Ocean Life 魚と海の生き物

- ☐ salmon（サケ）
- ☐ tuna（マグロ）
- ☐ eel（ウナギ）（イーゥ）
- ☐ whale（クジラ）
- ☐ dolphin（イルカ）
- ☐ seal（アザラシ）（スィーゥ）
- ☐ crab（カニ）（クゥレアブ）
- ☐ octopus（タコ）
- ☐ イカ squid（スクゥイド）
- ☐ エビ shrimp（シュゥリムプ）
- ☐ クラゲ jellyfish（ヂュエリフィシュ）
- ☐ サメ shark
- ☐ ヒトデ starfish（スターフィシュ）

付録

●Flowers and Trees 花や木

- ☐ tulip（チューリップ）
- ☐ sunflower（ひまわり）
- ☐ morning-glory（朝顔）
- ☐ cosmos（コスモス）
- ☐ pansy（パンジー）
- ☐ lily（ゆり）
- ☐ rose（バラ）
- ☐ cherry blossoms（桜）
- ☐ あやめ（しょうぶ） iris
- ☐ イチョウ gingko
- ☐ カーネーション carnation
- ☐ カエデ maple
- ☐ きんせんか marigold
- ☐ ここやし coconut
- ☐ 桜 cherry tree
- ☐ サボテン cactus
- ☐ 杉 cedar
- ☐ ダリア dahlia
- ☐ なつめやし date
- ☐ なら oak
- ☐ ハイビスカス hibiscus
- ☐ ヒヤシンス hyacinth
- ☐ 松 pine
- ☐ もみ fir
- ☐ 柳 willow
- ☐ らっぱすいせん daffodil
- ☐ ラン orchid

●Fruits and Vegetables 果物と野菜

- ☐ cabbage（キャベツ）
- ☐ cucumber（きゅうり）
- ☐ carrot（にんじん）
- ☐ tomato（トマト）
- ☐ potato（ジャガイモ）
- ☐ pineapple（パイナップル）
- ☐ strawberry（イチゴ）
- ☐ grapes（ぶどう）
- ☐ apple（りんご）
- ☐ banana（バナナ）
- ☐ orange（オレンジ）
- ☐ lemon（レモン）
- ☐ watermelon（スイカ）
- ☐ アスパラガス asparagus
- ☐ あんず apricot
- ☐ いちじく fig
- ☐ 枝豆 green soybeans
- ☐ 柿 persimmon
- ☐ かぼちゃ pumpkin
- ☐ カリフラワー cauliflower
- ☐ 栗 chestnut
- ☐ グレープフルーツ grapefruit
- ☐ ごぼう burdock root
- ☐ 小麦 wheat
- ☐ さくらんぼ cherry
- ☐ ざくろ pomegranate
- ☐ さつまいも sweet potato
- ☐ しょうが ginger
- ☐ セロリ celery
- ☐ 大根 daikon radish
- ☐ タケノコ bamboo shoot
- ☐ タマネギ onion
- ☐ 唐辛子 red pepper
- ☐ なし pear
- ☐ なす eggplant
- ☐ にんにく garlic
- ☐ ネギ leek
- ☐ 白菜 Chinese cabbage [bokchoy]
- ☐ パパイヤ papaya
- ☐ ピーマン green pepper
- ☐ ほうれん草 spinach
- ☐ マンゴー mango
- ☐ みかん mandarin orange
- ☐ メロン melon
- ☐ もやし bean sprouts
- ☐ ライム lime
- ☐ レタス lettuce
- ☐ れんこん lotus root

付録 4　動作を表す言葉（動詞）

☐ like　〜が好きだ，〜を好む

（例）I like cakes.

☐ play　（スポーツやゲームを）する

（例）He plays baseball every day.

☐ play　（楽器などを）演奏する

（例）He can play the piano very well.

☐ go (to) 〜　〜へ行く

（例）Taro goes to school by bicycle.

☐ come (to) 〜　〜へ来る

（例）Come here.

☐ study　〜を勉強する

（例）She studied hard last night.

☐ know　〜を知っている

（例）Do you know that girl?

☐ have　〜を持っている

（例）She has a nice car.

☐ have　〜がある，いる

（例）I have many friends.

動詞早わかりリスト

あ
- ☐ 遊ぶ play
- ☐ 歌う sing
- ☐ 選ぶ choose
- ☐ 覚える remember
- ☐ 折りたたむ fold
- ☐ 書く write
- ☐ 借りる borrow
- ☐ 感謝する thank
- ☐ 着る wear

さ
- ☐ さわる touch
- ☐ 招待する invite
- ☐ 尊敬する respect
- ☐ 立つ stand

- ☐ 歩く walk
- ☐ 受け取る receive
- ☐ 置く put
- ☐ 落ちる fall
- ☐ 折り曲げる bend
- ☐ 描く（絵を）draw
- ☐ 勝つ win
- ☐ 聞く listen (to) 〜
- ☐ 決める decide
- ☐ 〜したい want to 〜
- ☐ 信じる believe

た
- ☐ 滞在する stay
- ☐ 楽しむ enjoy

- ☐ 言う say
- ☐ 動く move
- ☐ 送る send
- ☐ 驚く be surprised
- ☐ 終わる finish
- ☐ 隠す hide
- ☐ 考える think
- ☐ 聞こえる hear
- ☐ 加える add
- ☐ 閉める close
- ☐ 住む live
- ☐ 尋ねる ask
- ☐ 食べる eat

- ☐ 意味する mean
- ☐ 運転する drive
- ☐ 押す push
- ☐ 泳ぐ swim

か
- ☐ 買う buy
- ☐ 貸す lend
- ☐ 感じる feel
- ☐ 切る cut
- ☐ こわす break
- ☐ しゃべる talk
- ☐ 座る sit
- ☐ 訪ねる visit
- ☐ 試す try